THE OFFICIAL HAMMERS

WEST HAM UNITED
LONDON

YEARBOOK

2016/2017

Written by twocan
Contributor: Peter Rogers
A TWOCAN PUBLICATION
©2016. Published by twocan under licence from West Ham United FC.

ISBN 978-1-909872-91-2

CONTENTS

FIXTURES 2016/17

AUGUST
Monday	15	Chelsea	A
Sunday	21	Bournemouth	H
Sunday	28	Manchester City	A

SEPTEMBER
Saturday	10	Watford	H
Saturday	17	West Brom	A
Wednesday	21	Accrington Stanley	H	EFL Cup 3
Sunday	25	Southampton	H

OCTOBER
Saturday	1	Middlesbrough	H
Saturday	15	Crystal Palace	A
Saturday	22	Sunderland	H
Wednesday	26	Chelsea	H	EFL Cup 4
Sunday	30	Everton	A

NOVEMBER
Saturday	5	Stoke City	H
Saturday	19	Tottenham Hotspur	A
Sunday	27	Manchester United	A

DECEMBER
Saturday	3	Arsenal	H
Sunday	11	Liverpool	A
Wednesday	14	Burnley	H
Saturday	17	Hull City	H
Monday	26	Swansea City	A
Saturday	31	Leicester City	A

JANUARY
Monday	2	Manchester United	H
Saturday	7			FA Cup Round 3
Saturday	14	Crystal Palace	H
Saturday	21	Middlesbrough	A
Saturday	28			FA Cup Round 4

FEBRUARY
Wednesday	1	Manchester City	H
Saturday	4	Southampton	A
Saturday	11	West Brom	H
Saturday	18			FA Cup Round 5
Saturday	25	Watford	A

MARCH
Saturday	4	Chelsea	H
Saturday	11	Bournemouth	A	FA Cup Round 6
Saturday	18	Leicester City	H

APRIL
Saturday	1	Hull City	A
Tuesday	4	Arsenal	A
Saturday	8	Swansea City	H
Saturday	15	Sunderland	A
Saturday	22	Everton	H	FA Cup Semi-Final
Saturday	29	Stoke City	A

MAY
Saturday	6	Tottenham Hotspur	H
Saturday	13	Liverpool	H
Sunday	21	Burnley	A
Saturday	27	Everton	H	FA Cup Final

WEST HAM UN

umbro

betway

TED 2016/2017

SECOND ROW: Tom Taylor, Julian Dicks, Alvaro Arbeloa, Arthur Masuaku, Darren Randolph, Adrian, Raphael Spiegel, Cheikhou Kouyate, Andre Ayew, Chris Woods, Jamie Osman. **FRONT ROW:** Jack Lamb-Wilson, Tamim Khanbhai, Aaron Cresswell, Michail Antonio, Mark Noble, Edin Terzic, Slaven Bilic, Nikola Jurcevic, Miljenko Rak, Winston Reid, Dimitri Payet, Manuel Lanzini, Will Storey, Eamon Swift.

Of the many successful on-field partnerships down the years at West Ham, there are not many that have matched the magical moments such as those created by midfield maestros Alan Devonshire and Trevor Brooking.

DOUBLE DEVONSHIRE

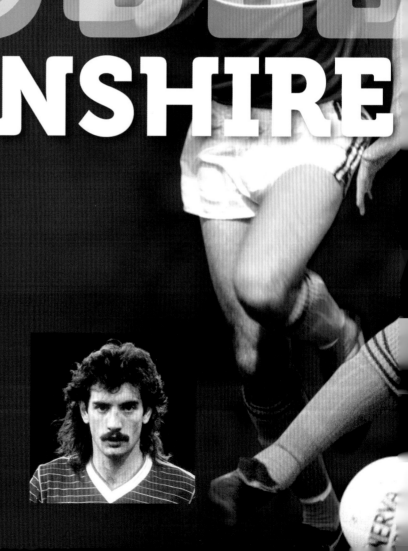

A true Hammers icon, Brooking was born in Barking on 2 October 1948 and the double FA Cup winner's name is synonymous with the club, having later served as a Director and also having two brief spells as caretaker manager.

Brooking had been successfully pulling the strings in the West Ham midfielder for almost ten years before Devonshire arrived at the club. During that period, Brooking had won the first of his two FA Cup winners' medals as the Hammers overcame Fulham at Wembley in 1975 thanks to an Alan Taylor brace. Brooking had also at that stage landed two of his five 'Hammer of the Year' award.

Devonshire, born in Middlesex on 13 April 1956, had a tricky route into the professional game after twice being turned away by Crystal Palace, before heading into non-league football. It was while plying his trade for Southall, he was spotted by the Hammers and signed in 1976 for a fee of £5,000 which has constantly led to him being referred to as West Ham's best-ever buy.

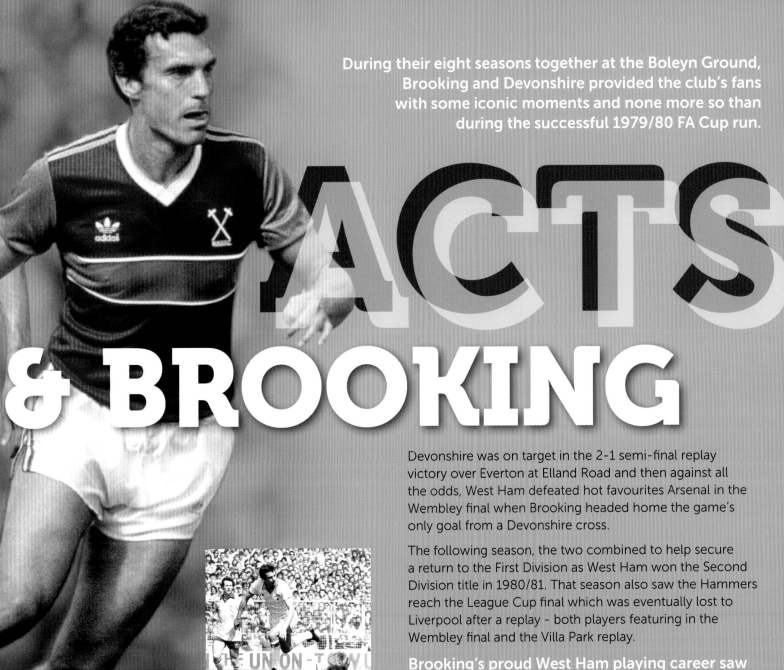

During their eight seasons together at the Boleyn Ground, Brooking and Devonshire provided the club's fans with some iconic moments and none more so than during the successful 1979/80 FA Cup run.

ACTS
& BROOKING

Devonshire was on target in the 2-1 semi-final replay victory over Everton at Elland Road and then against all the odds, West Ham defeated hot favourites Arsenal in the Wembley final when Brooking headed home the game's only goal from a Devonshire cross.

The following season, the two combined to help secure a return to the First Division as West Ham won the Second Division title in 1980/81. That season also saw the Hammers reach the League Cup final which was eventually lost to Liverpool after a replay - both players featuring in the Wembley final and the Villa Park replay.

Brooking's proud West Ham playing career saw him make 643 appearances for the club and score 102 goals between 1967 and 1984.

Devonshire played in a total of 448 games for the club, scoring 32 goals before ending his playing days at Watford.

9

Ahead of the historic debut season at London Stadium, West Ham United began their preparations for the 2016/17 season with an exciting two-game tour of the United States and a challenging three-match training camp in Austria.

After securing a seventh place finish in the Premier League, which gained entry to the qualifying stages of the Europa League, Slaven Bilic's men also faced Juventus in the official opening of London Stadium ahead of the all-important Premier League season opener at Chelsea.

With Euro 2016 still in full swing when the Hammers jetted off to the States in early July, those who had been involved in the tournament or were still fighting for international glory in France were not included in the travelling party. As a result a number of fringe players from the Development squad were given their opportunity to travel with the first team squad for warm weather training and friendly fixtures against Seattle Sounders and Carolina RailHawks.

A crowd of 38,385 saw the Hammers go down 3-0 to MLS side Seattle Sounders on Tuesday 5 July at CenturyLink Field in Seattle. The Hammers were beaten courtesy of a 42nd-minute penalty won and converted by Sounders striker Herculez Gomez after Adrian had brought down the former United States international, and a quick-fire second-half double from leading goalscorer Jordan Morris.

Less than a week into their preparations for the new season, boss Bilic used 21 players in this fixture handing debuts to the impressive Sofiane Feghouli, Havard Nordtveit and youngsters Antonio Martinez and Domingos Quina.

The second and final match of the tour saw an eventful 2-2 draw with Carolina RailHawks on 12 July at the WakeMed Soccer Park in Cary, North Carolina.

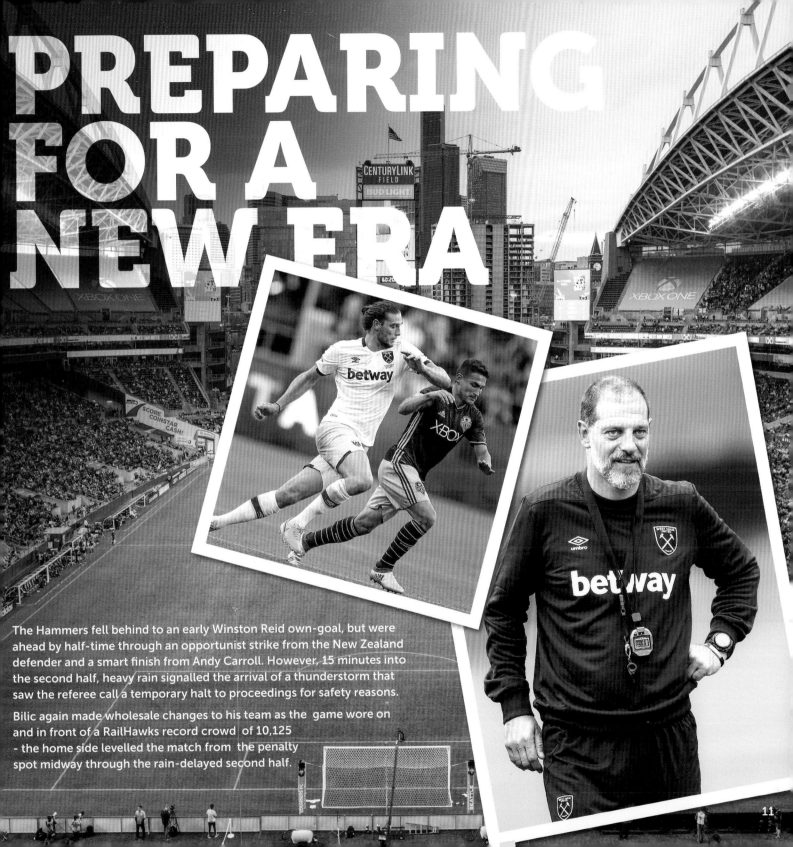

PREPARING FOR A NEW ERA

The Hammers fell behind to an early Winston Reid own-goal, but were ahead by half-time through an opportunist strike from the New Zealand defender and a smart finish from Andy Carroll. However, 15 minutes into the second half, heavy rain signalled the arrival of a thunderstorm that saw the referee call a temporary halt to proceedings for safety reasons.

Bilic again made wholesale changes to his team as the game wore on and in front of a RailHawks record crowd of 10,125 - the home side levelled the match from the penalty spot midway through the rain-delayed second half.

11

The club's three-match training camp in Austria certainly proved to be a mixed bag result-wise as Bilic saw his squad draw, lose and win against European opposition over a four-day period.

After ending the United States tour with a 2-2 draw, West Ham began their spell in Austria in the same fashion as goals from Mark Noble and Ashley Fletcher secured a 2-2 draw with Czech side FC Slovacko on the 19 July.

The following day the Hammers suffered a 3-0 defeat to Russian club Rubin Kazan before facing one of manager Bilic's former clubs Karlsruher SC on 23 July. Goals from Andy Carroll, Sofiane Feghouli and Ashley Fletcher proved enough to give the Hammers a 3-0 victory over their German opponents and end a useful spell on a winning note.

Next up was the commencement of the Europa League campaign and West Ham were left with work to do in the second leg of their UEFA Europa League third qualifying round tie against NK Domzale after falling to a 2-1 defeat in Slovenia on Thursday 28 July.

A Matic Crnic double gave the hosts a first leg advantage despite Mark Noble's successful penalty conversion in the first half. This narrow defeat certainly set things up perfectly for the club's much anticipated opening game at London Stadium on Thursday 4 August.

In front of a crowd of 54,000 a Cheikhou Kouyate double and a maiden strike for Sofiane Feghouli crowned a historic night for West Ham United at the new Stadium as the side secured progression to the play-off stages of the Europa League.

Slovenian side NK Domzale were downed by Senegal midfielder Kouyate's first half brace before Feghouli struck in the final ten minutes to record a 4-2 aggregate victory over two legs.

On Sunday 7 August the club officially opened the new Stadium with a prestigious fixture against Italian giants Juventus in the Betway Cup. The occasion was marked by an opening ceremony before the kick-off which was a fitting tribute to the Hammers' new home.

Andy Carroll showed his qualities once again ahead of the new Premier League season with two goals but future Hammer Simone Zaza grabbed a late winner to help the Italian champions come away with a 3-2 victory.

Juventus raced into a two-goal lead following early goals from Paulo Dybala and Mario Mandzukic. But Carroll, who was a constant threat to the Juventus defence, helped the Hammers get back into the game with two goals either side of half-time.

Nearly 54,000 fans turned out in their numbers once again and were thrilled to see Dimitri Payet make his first appearance at the new Stadium during the second half.

Despite beginning the 2016/17 Premier League campaign with a narrow 2-1 defeat at Chelsea, West Ham marked their opening league game at London Stadium with a victory.

Michail Antonio stole the headlines as he scored a dramatic late winner to hand West Ham their first ever Premier League victory at their new home with a 1-0 win over Bournemouth.

Antonio wrote his name into the record books when he became the first ever scorer for the club at their new home in the top flight and it was a moment to remember for the talented winger.

The game looked to be heading for a goalless draw until Gokhan Tore picked up the ball down the left hand side on 84 minutes and played in a superb cross towards the far post.

Antonio rose above the Bournemouth defence and directed an unstoppable header into the back of the net to hand West Ham a memorable first victory in the top flight this season.

THANK YOU FOUNDERS

15

SPOT
THE SEASON

The club was under the management of John Lyall

Also in this season, Wimbledon finished sixth in the First Division in only their tenth season as a football League club, newly-promoted Norwich City grabbed fifth spot, the First Division title was won by a manager who left his club at the end of the season to try his luck in Spain,

...and Manchester City were relegated after losing to the Hammers 2-0 at the Boleyn Ground on the final day of the season.

Billy Bonds was voted Hammer of the Year

ANSWER ON PAGE 82

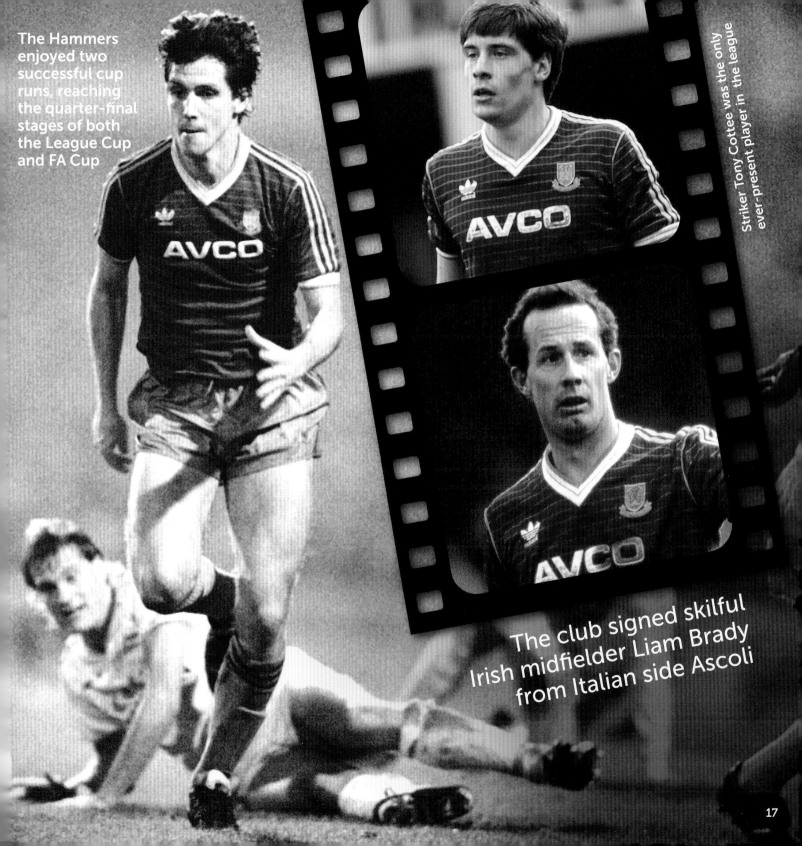

The Hammers enjoyed two successful cup runs, reaching the quarter-final stages of both the League Cup and FA Cup

Striker Tony Cottee was the only ever-present player in the league

The club signed skilful Irish midfielder Liam Brady from Italian side Ascoli

17

PREMIER LEAGUE SQUAD 16/17

1

Darren **Randolph**

POSITION: Goalkeeper
DATE OF BIRTH: 12 May 1987
PLACE OF BIRTH: Bray, Ireland

Republic of Ireland goalkeeper Darren Randolph joined the Hammers in the summer of 2015, following the expiration of his contract with Championship club Birmingham City.

A much-travelled and experienced 'keeper, Randolph began his career with Charlton Athletic and gained a plethora of experience with loan spells at Welling United, Accrington Stanley, Gillingham, Bury and Hereford. After leaving the Valley, he took in a spell north of the border with Motherwell before joining Birmingham City in May 2013.

Randolph proved to be an excellent understudy to Adrian in 2015/16 and although Premier League opportunities were hard to come by, he featured regularly in the cup competitions for Slaven Bilic's side.

When called on to deputise for Adrian in Premier League fixtures, he registered a clean sheet in the Hammers long-awaited victory at Anfield and he also played in the final game at the Boleyn Ground. As the Republic's first-choice stopper, he played in all four fixtures for his country in Euro 2016.

Winston **Reid**

POSITION: Defender
DATE OF BIRTH: 3 July 1998
PLACE OF BIRTH: Auckland, New Zealand

Winston Reid was recruited from Danish side FC Midtjylland in 2011 and the New Zealander has become an impressive performer for the Hammers with the ability to operate at right-back or as a central-defender.

Reid moved to Denmark at the age of just ten and won international youth honours with the Danes before switching international allegiance back to the country of his birth. His decision to do so was rewarded as he started all three of New Zealand's 2010 World Cup matches in South Africa.

His Hammers debut came in a 3-0 reverse to Aston Villa on 14 August 2010 and he made seven Premier League appearances as the club suffered relegation. However, Reid became a regular face in the side during the 2011/12 Championship campaign when the Hammers regained their Premier League status via the Play-Offs. 2012/13 was another memorable season for Reid. His outstanding performances at the heart of the defence were rewarded with him receiving the prestigious Hammer of the Year award.

In March 2016 he committed his future to the club with a new long-term contract and he took the mantle of scoring the final goal at the Boleyn Ground, when his 80th minute header sealed a 3-2 victory over Manchester United on 10 May 2016.

Aaron **Cresswell**

POSITION: Defender
DATE OF BIRTH: 15 December 1989
PLACE OF BIRTH: Liverpool

Left-back Aaron Cresswell joined the Hammers from Ipswich Town in July 2014.

The Liverpool-born defender began his career at Tranmere Rovers where a series of polished performances resulted in a switch from Prenton Park to Portman Road in 2011.

After arriving at the Boleyn Ground he swiftly made the left-back berth his own and was the only outfield player to feature in every minute of the club's 2014/15 Premier League campaign. A consistent performer with a real appetite to get forward and support the attack, his displays won the seal of approval among the Hammers faithful who voted him Hammer of the Year during his debut season with the club.

The 2015/16 season saw Cresswell continue to be one of the first names on new manager Slaven Bilic's teamsheet as he played a vital role in helping the club to a seventh-placed finish in the Premier League. Sadly, Cresswell suffered knee ligament damage in the pre-season match against Karlsrusher SC and was sidelined, returning to the side for the 1-0 victory over Crystal Palace at Selhurst Park on 15 October.

4

Havard **Nordtveit**

POSITION: Midfielder
DATE OF BIRTH: 21 June 1990
PLACE OF BIRTH: Vats, Norway

Defensive midfielder Havard Nordtveit joined the Hammers in July 2016 following the completion of the Norwegian international's contract with German side Borussia Monchengladbach.

The tough-tackling midfielder began his career in Norway with Haugesund and became the youngest player to represent the club when he made his debut. Aged just 17, he joined Arsenal in 2007 and despite captaining the Gunners' reserve side, he failed to make at first-team appearance for the club.

Loan moves to Salamanca, Lillestrom and FC Nuremberg all provided excellent experience, before he departed the Emirates for Borussia Monchengladbach in 2011. He swiftly established himself as a key player for Borussia Monchengladbach and made over 150 league appearances before completing his switch to West Ham.

He made his debut for the club is the Europa League tie away to Domzale before enjoying a winning home debut as the Hammers cruised past Domzale 3-0 at London Stadium, to turn around a 2-1 first-leg defeat and win the tie 4-2 on aggregate.

Alvaro **Arbeloa**

POSITION: Defender
DATE OF BIRTH: 17 January 1983
PLACE OF BIRTH: Salamanca, Spain

On the final day of summer transfer window, the Hammers secured the services of the experienced and versatile Spanish defender Alvaro Arbeloa on a one-year contract.

Arbeloa arrived at London Stadium with a highly impressive CV that includes a FIFA World Cup triumph and two UEFA European Championships successes with Spain at international level. The 33-year-old can also boast a host of club honours, including two UEFA Champions Leagues triumphs with Spanish giants Real Madrid.

In between two spells with Real Madrid, Arbeloa sandwiched in spells with both Deportivo La Coruna and Liverpool, where he made 66 Premier League appearances.

Upon his arrival at West Ham, Arbeloa expressed his enthusiasm for the Premier League, working with manager Slaven Bilic and playing in front of packed crowds at London Stadium. With a wealth experience to call upon, Arbeloa looks set to be an impressive addition to the Hammers squad both on the pitch and off, where his advice and guidance could be invaluable to the club's younger players.

5

7

Sofiane **Feghouli**

POSITION: Midfielder
DATE OF BIRTH: 26 December 1989
PLACE OF BIRTH: Levallois-Perrett, France

Algerian international Sofiane Feghouli arrived at the club in July 2016, having agreed a three-year deal with the Hammers following the conclusion of his contract at Valencia.

Aged 26, Feghouli is a French-born Algerian winger who can also operate in a more central attacking role and is sure to excite the Hammers faithful over the coming season.

He began his career in France with Grenoble where his impressive attacking performances led to a move to Spanish giants Valencia in 2010. A full Algerian international with 40 caps and eleven goals to his name, Feghouli ended his Valencia career having made 202 appearances for the club and netting 31 times.

Feghouli made his Hammers debut in the away leg of the Europa League tie with Domzale. He then etched his name into Hammers history by adding his name to the scoresheet in the first game at the new London Stadium in the return leg. A thigh injury sustained in the pre-season friendly with Juventus then resulted on a spell in the treatment room.

Cheikhou **Kouyate**

POSITION: Midfielder
DATE OF BIRTH: 21 December 1989
PLACE OF BIRTH: Daker, Senegal

Following his arrival at West Ham in June 2014, Senegalese international midfielder Cheikhou Kouyate has become an integral part of the Hammers team, as his energetic displays have won him a host of admirers.

Kouyate moved to Europe at the age of 15 when he joined the academy at FC Brussels, but made his name during an immensely-successful six-year spell with Anderlecht.

A popular character off the pitch and with Europa League and Champions League experience to call upon, he wasted little time in making his mark at the Boleyn Ground. Kouyate produced a number of sensational performances during his first two seasons with the club and chipped in with vital goals too. Such has his importance to the team become, that his absence while on international duty, has certainly been felt.

He cemented his name into West Ham folklore at the start of the 2016/17 season when he became the first player to score at the new London Stadium, when he struck just eight minutes into the Hammers 3-0 Europa League victory over Domzale.

Andy **Carroll**

POSITION: Forward
DATE OF BIRTH: 6 January 1989
PLACE OF BIRTH: Gateshead

9

Powerful frontman Andy Carroll initially joined the Hammers on loan from Liverpool in August 2012 before agreeing a permanent switch in May 2013 - for a then club record fee.

Having begun his career with Newcastle United and progressing through the youth and reserve ranks at St James' Park, Carroll had earned the reputation as one of the country's most feared strikers, with his physical presence and eye for goal often labelling him unplayable by opponents. His form for the Magpies won him a £35 million move to Liverpool in January 2011, but despite a memorable FA Cup semi-final goal against Everton, Carroll was unable to recreate his Newcastle form at Anfield.

Since joining the Hammers, Carroll has produced some outstanding displays and has become a firm fans favourite. However, his time with the club has been blighted by a series of injuries, that have subsequently prevented him from producing the goalscoring performances that he and all Hammers fans crave.

The 2015/16 campaign saw him chip in with nine Premier League goal including a memorable hat-trick against Arsenal in April 2016.

Manuel **Lanzini**

POSITION: Midfielder
DATE OF BIRTH: 15 February 1993
PLACE OF BIRTH: Ituzaingo, Argentina

Argentinean midfielder Manuel Lanzini joined the Hammers in the summer of 2015 on a season-long loan deal from UAE side Al-Jazira.

Blessed with exceptional close control and a real desire to run at opponents, Lanzini proved a massive hit at the Boleyn Ground, as his debut season in England ended with 31 appearances and a highly-impressive seven goals.

He immediately hit the ground running with a goalscoring debut in the Europa League against Astra Girugiu and marked his first Premier League start with a goal in the memorable 3-0 triumph at Anfield. Injury ruled him out for a lengthy period at the start of 2016, but he returned to the side with goalscoring displays in the London derby fixtures against Chelsea and Crystal Palace.

The deal to bring Lanzini to West Ham carried an option for the move to become permanent and such was the impression he made during the 2015/16 season that the club exercised this option and Lanzini became a permanent Hammer in July 2016.

PREMIER LEAGUE SQUAD 16/17

11

Simone **Zaza**

POSITION: Forward
DATE OF BIRTH: 25 June 1991
PLACE OF BIRTH: Policoro, Italy

The Hammers signed Italy striker Simone Zaza from Juventus on a season-long loan deal in August 2016.

A powerful striker with an impressive goal-to-games ratio, Zaza began his career with Atalanta, where he progressed through the club's youth system to go on and play for the first team in Serie A.

After only three appearances for Atalanta, his potential was spotted by Sampdoria, who he joined on a four-year contract. Zaza made only two first team appearances for Sampdoria, but enjoyed loan spells at Juve Stabia, Viareggio and Ascoli. His time at Ascoli was particularly successful as he scored 18 goals in 36 matches, earning the forward a move to Sassuolo where he found the back of the net 21 times in 69 games.

At the start of the 2015/16 campaign, Zaza joined Juventus and played for Italy at UEFA Euro 2016. His arrival at London Stadium sparked a great deal of excitement among the West Ham fans, who will be hopeful he can recreate his Ascoli form in a Hammers shirt in 2016/17.

Adrian

POSITION: Goalkeeper
DATE OF BIRTH: 3 January 1987
PLACE OF BIRTH: Seville, Spain

Goalkeeper Adrian San Miguel del Castillo, known simply as Adrian, has become a firm favourite with the West Ham faithful since joining the club from Real Betis in July 2013.

The giant stopper has made the goalkeeper's shirt his own with a string of eye-catching performances over the past three seasons and has now amassed over 100 appearances for the club.

He carried on his superb form from the previous season, keeping a clean sheet in the 2015/16 opening day victory at Arsenal. After suffering a three-match suspension following his red card in the 2-1 defeat to Leicester, Adrian returned to the side for the impressive 2-1 triumph away to Manchester City.

His form was rewarded with a new longer-term contract in October 2015 and his reliable performances and clean sheets proved vital as the Hammers recorded a seventh-place Premier League finish and secured European football once again.

The new 2016/17 season began with a career highlight, as his fine club form was recognised with an international call-up. He was included in the Spanish squad for a friendly with Belgium and a World Cup 2018 qualifier with Liechtenstein.

13

14

Pedro **Obiang**

POSITION: Midfielder
DATE OF BIRTH: 27 March 1992
PLACE OF BIRTH: Alcala de Henares, Spain

All-action midfielder Pedro Obiang joined the Irons from Sampdoria in the summer of 2015 and made a big impression at the Boleyn Ground in his first season with the club.

A Spanish Under-21 international, Obiang was brought up in Madrid and played youth football for Atletico Madrid, but opted to leave his homeland and join Sampdoria at the tender age of 16.

After playing over 130 league games for Sampdoria, his Hammers career did not get off to the best of starts, a hamstring injury in pre-season ruling him out of action at the start of the season. His debut came at home to Leicester City on 15 August 2016 and he went on to feature in the impressive early season victories away to Liverpool and Manchester City.

Obiang made a total of 30 appearances for the club in all competitions last season and late substitute appearances have seen him feature in both the first Europa League and first Premier League games at the new London Stadium in 2016/17.

Diafra **Sakho**

POSITION: Forward

DATE OF BIRTH: 24 December 1989

PLACE OF BIRTH: Guediawaye, Senegal

Senegalese forward Diafra Sakho joined the Hammers from French side FC Metz in August 2014.

After spending his entire professional career with Metz, he agreed a four-year deal with West Ham and enjoyed a highly-impressive debut season for the club in 2014/15. A quick, strong and all-round quality athlete, Sakho soon impressed all at the Boleyn Ground and ended the campaign with very respectable 12 goals from 26 appearances.

Sakho began the 2015/16 season in a similar vein to how he ended the previous campaign, helping himself to two goals in the 3-0 Europa League victory over FA Lusitans at the Boleyn Ground. Premier League goals against Liverpool, Manchester City and Norwich City followed, before injury ruled him out for a three -month spell in the middle of the season.

He eventually returned to the side in March 2016 as the Hammers enjoyed a London derby triumph over Spurs. He managed two further goals before the end of the season, with his last goal of the season arriving in the historic final game at the Boleyn Ground against Manchester United.

16

Mark **Noble**

POSITION: Midfielder
DATE OF BIRTH: 8 May 1987
PLACE OF BIRTH: Canning Town

Inspirational captain Mark Noble is the club's longest serving player among the current squad, having made his Hammers debut back in August 2004 in a 2-0 League Cup triumph over Southend United at the Boleyn Ground.

Idolised by the Hammers faithful, Noble was voted Hammer of the Year in both 2011/12 and 2013/14. His all-action midfield displays, coupled with an exquisite range of passing skills, continue to impress season after season and have seen him acknowledged as a true Hammers legend.

Noble's loyalty to the club was rewarded with a memorable testimonial fixture at the Boleyn Ground in March 2016 when the Hammers took on a side of West Ham United all-stars in front of a crowd of 35,036.

Once again the 2015/16 season saw Noble at his very best, chipping in with seven goals from his 46 appearances in the Hammers engine room. The popular midfielder was swiftly among the goals as the 2016/17 season got underway, with two goals in the club's Europa League campaign.

Gokhan Tore

POSITION: Midfielder
DATE OF BIRTH: 20 January 1992
PLACE OF BIRTH: Cologne, Germany

Hammers boss Slaven Bilic knows all about Turkish midfielder Gokhan Tore, having managed the 24-year-old when the two were at Besiktas.

A full Turkish international, Tore joined the club in July 2016 on a season-long loan deal from Besiktas with an option to purchase the player at a later date on a permanent basis.

German-born Tore spent time with both Bayer Leverkusen and Chelsea as a youngster, before sampling first-team football with Hamburg. In 2012/13, Tore joined Rubin Kazan in Russia, but made only seven appearances before moving on to Besiktas. He enjoyed a useful first season scoring four goals in the Super Lig. In his second campaign with Besiktas he was managed by Bilic and in his third, Tore helped his side win the division.

Delighted to reunite with his former boss, Tore made his Hammers debut on the opening week of Premier League fixtures, away to Chelsea.

19

James Collins

POSITION: Defender
DATE OF BIRTH: 23 August 1983
PLACE OF BIRTH: Newport

Now in his second spell with the Hammers, Wales international defender James Collins made 25 first team appearances in 2015/16, before enjoying a memorable Euro 2016 campaign with his country.

A powerful and fully-committed central defender, Collins began his career with Cardiff City before joining the Hammers for the first time in 2005. In his first spell at the Boleyn Ground he helped the club reach the FA Cup final in 2006 and battle successfully against relegation in 2007. After three years with Aston Villa, Collins joined the club for a second time in August 2012.

Always guaranteed to give 100 per cent to the cause, Collins played a vital role in helping the Hammers secure a seventh-place Premier League finish in 2015/16 and produced particularly impressive displays in the London derby victories over Crystal Palace and Chelsea. He also turned in memorable performances to help the side record clean sheets against Liverpool and Spurs.

The summer of 2016 saw Collins link-up with his Welsh teammates in France for Euro 2016 where he featured in Wales' historic victory over Belgium before Chris Coleman's men bowed out at the semi-final stage to eventual winners Portugal.

After a terrific debut campaign in the Premier League with Swansea City last season, West Ham completed the signing of Ghanaian international forward Andre Ayew for a club record fee in the summer of 2016.

The son of three-time African Footballer of the Year Abedi Ayew, football is clearly in the family genes, with brothers Ibrahim and Jordan also plying their trade in the professional game.

Ayew began his career in Ghana before joining Marseille and enjoyed loan spells with Lorient and Arles-Avignon before establishing himself in the Marseille side and where he made over 200 appearances and scored 60 goals before making the move to South Wales.

He marked his debut for the Swans with a goal against Chelsea and went on to fire home 12 goals from 35 games while at the Liberty Stadium. He made his Hammers bow in the opening Premier League fixture away to Chelsea.

Andre **Ayew**

POSITION: Forward

DATE OF BIRTH: 17 December 1989

PLACE OF BIRTH: Seclin, France

Angelo **Ogbonna**

POSITION: Defender
DATE OF BIRTH: 23 May 1988
PLACE OF BIRTH: Cassino, Italy

Italian defender Angelo Ogbonna was a runner-up at Euro 2012 with his country and joined the Hammers in July 2015 from Juventus.

A strong and powerful central defender who also has the flexibility to operate at left-back, Ogbonna won back-to-back Italian tittles with Juventus prior to his arrival in London.

He enjoyed a wining debut as the Hammers triumphed 2-0 at Arsenal on the opening day, but suffered a hamstring injury against Newcastle in September which ruled him out for several weeks. Returning to the starting line-up against West Bromwich Albion in November, he played a starring role as the team went on an eight-match unbeaten run.

With a penalty shootout looming in the FA Cup Fourth Round Replay against Liverpool at the Boleyn Ground, Ogbonna picked the perfect time to head home his first goal in Claret and Blue to seal a memorable 2-1 extra-time triumph that sealed a fifth round trip to Blackburn Rovers.

Sam **Byram**

POSITION: Defender
DATE OF BIRTH: 16 September 1993
PLACE OF BIRTH: Thurrock

The Hammers faced stiff competition for promising young defender Sam Byram before landing his signature during the January 2016 transfer window.

A pacy right-back who is swift in the tackle, Byram gained the reputation as one of the brightest young defenders around as he progressed through the academy ranks at Leeds United. He was handed his first-team debut by Neil Warnock in a League Cup tie at home to Shrewsbury Town in August 2012. He went on to play a total of 143 games for Yorkshire outfit, scoring ten goals.

He joined the Hammers on 20 January 2016 for an undisclosed fee and agreed a four-and-a-half year contract, the club demonstrating its desire to recruit the best young talent available.

A memorable debut saw Byram thrust into the limelight as he appeared as an early substitute for the injured Carl Jenkinson, during an eventful 2-2 draw with Manchester City at the Boleyn Ground. He made a total of four first-team appearances last season - all of which the Hammers remained unbeaten.

Ashley **Fletcher**

POSITION: Forward
DATE OF BIRTH: 2 October 1995
PLACE OF BIRTH: Keighley

Recruited from Premier League rivals Manchester United, young forward Ashley Fletcher joined the Hammers in the summer of 2016 following the expiry of his contract at Old Trafford.

Born in Keighley, Fletcher began his schoolboy career with Bolton Wanderers aged nine, but joined Manchester United at the age of 13 and signed his first professional contract in May 2014.

Despite a useful goals-to-games-ratio and an impressive strike partnership with James Wilson for the Red Devils' U21 side, Fletcher found first-team opportunities tough to come by at Manchester United. As a result he joined League One Barnsley in January 2016 in search of first-team action.

Fletcher proved to be an outstanding success for Paul Heckingbottom's Tykes, who climbed the League One table to reach the end-of-season Play-Offs. He netted a total of nine goals in 27 appearances for Barnsley including a goal in the Wembley Play-Off final victory over Millwall, as the South Yorkshire side sealed promotion to the Championship.

Following his success at Oakwell, Fletcher was offered a contract to stay at Old Trafford, but opted to join the Hammers and made his debut in the UEFA Europa League victory over NK Domzale when he replaced Andy Carroll in the closing stages of a 3-0 win.

26

Arthur **Masuaku**

POSITION: Defender
DATE OF BIRTH: 11 November 1993
PLACE OF BIRTH: Lille, France

After enjoying two title-winning seasons in Greece with Olympiacos, highly-rated young French defender Arthur Masusku joined the Hammers in August 2016 for a fee of £6.2 million.

Born in Lille, Masuaku began his youth career in his home city, before spells with RC Lens and Valenciennes led to his move to Greece in July 2014.

He arrived at London Stadium full of confidence having helped Olympiacos to back-to-back Greek Superleague titles - the 2015/16 campaign saw Masuaku and his teammates win an incredible 28 of their 30 league fixtures.

He made his full Hammers debut on the opening week of the Premier League season at Chelsea and was once again in the starting line-up for the historic first home league fixture at London Stadium against Bournemouth. His home debut was great success with the Hammers recording a victory as Masusku and his defensive colleagues registered their first clean-sheet of the campaign.

24

27

Dimitri **Payet**

POSITION: Midfielder
DATE OF BIRTH: 29 March 1987
PLACE OF BIRTH: Saint-Pierre, France

Recruited from Marseille, French international midfield playmaker Dimitri Payet was the Hammers star signing in the summer of 2015.

The immensely-talented Frenchman certainly repaid manager Slaven Bilic's faith in him as he proceeded to be the true driving force behind the club's successful 2015/16 season, that ended with a seventh-placed finish and qualification for the 2016/17 Europa League.

Payet contributed a host of memorable moments during 2015/16 and he ended the season with 12 goals and 15 assists for his teammates in all competitions. His Premier League adventure began at the Emirates on the opening weekend of the season as he set up Cheikhou Kouyate's for the opening goal in the 2-0 win at Arsenal. A first Premier League goal arrived against Leicester City and strikes against Newcastle United (two), Sunderland and Crystal Palace followed before injury ruled him out for seven games in November and December.

However, he returned from his lay off to help inspire a 2-0 victory over Liverpool before getting back on the scoresheet with a trademark free-kick away to Bournemouth. He also crashed home an unstoppable free-kick in the FA Cup tie with Manchester United at Old Trafford and ended the season with the Hammer of the Year award.

28

Jonathan **Calleri**

POSITION: Forward
DATE OF BIRTH: 23 September 1993
PLACE OF BIRTH: Buenos Aires

Exciting forward Jonathan Calleri joined the Hammers on loan in August 2016 and made his debut in the Europa League match with Astra Giurgiu.

Born in the Argentinean capital of Buenos Aires, Calleri began his career with second division side, All Boys. An impressive goals-to-games ratio soon alerted some of the biggest names in South America and in 2014 he joined Argentine giants Boca Juniors. He scored an impressive 23 goals in 59 matches for the side before joining Uruguayan side Deportivo Maldonado and immediately being loaned to Brazilian side Sao Paulo where he fired home 16 goals in 31 matches.

Calleri was unfortunate not to mark his Hammers debut with a goal as he twice had efforts cleared off the line against Astra Giurgiu. He almost added his name to the scoresheet in the first Premier League match at London Stadium, but his late effort went only inches wide of the Bournemouth post.

This talented forward is well aware of the impact his Argentine compatriot Carlos Tevez made with the Hammers and will be aiming to follow in his footsteps during the 2016/17 season.

Michail **Antonio**

POSITION: Midfielder
DATE OF BIRTH: 28 March 1990
PLACE OF BIRTH: Wandsworth

West Ham United competed the signing of attacking midfielder Michail Antonio from Championship side Nottingham Forest in September 2015 and the London-born winger enjoyed a highly-successful debut season with the Hammers.

Antonio began his career in non-league football with Tooting & Mitcham before joining Reading in 2008. During his time with the Royals, Antonio had something of a nomadic existence with a host of loan moves, gaining useful Football League experience.

After successful spells with Sheffield Wednesday and Forest, his switch to the Hammers offered him the chance to prove his worth at the highest level and Antonio has certainly made the most of his opportunity.

His Hammers debut came in the memorable 2-1 victory at Manchester City on 19 September 2016, with his first goal for the club arriving in a 2-1 success against Southampton. He enjoyed an impressive run of form when he netted consecutive winners at home to Sunderland and Spurs, before then adding his name to the scoresheet in the 3-2 triumph at Everton. He netted nine goals last season and began the new 2016/17 season in fine style by scoring the first Premier League goal at London Stadium. His form since joining the Hammers resulted in him being named in both Sam Allardyce and Gareth Southgate's first England squads.

30

Attacking midfielder Edimilson Fernandes joined West Ham United in August 2016 from Swiss Super League side FC Sion and agreed a four-year deal at the Stadium.

Football is certainly in the family blood with Fernandes being the cousin of former Manchester City midfielder Gelson, as well as ex-Everton man Manuel and former Sunderland man Cabra. He began his career with his hometown club, initially joining FC Sion at the age of eleven and making his first-team debut six years later.

In his three years as a professional at Sion, Fernandes made 65 appearances for the club and his impressive form won him international recognition with Switzerland at Under-21 level.

He made his Hammers debut in the EFL Cup victory over Accrington Stanley before going on to taste Premier League action with late substitute appearances at home to Southampton and away to Crystal Palace, before impressing during his home league debut in the victory over Sunderland.

Edimilson **Fernandes**

POSITION: Midfielder
DATE OF BIRTH: 15 April 1996
PLACE OF BIRTH: Sion, Switzerland

34

Raphael **Spiegel**

POSITION: Goalkeeper
DATE OF BIRTH: 19 December 1992
PLACE OF BIRTH: Ruttenen, Switzerland

Promising young Swiss goalkeeper Raphael Spiegel arrived at West Ham United in 2012 and enjoyed a successful season with the Under-21 Development Squad in 2015/16.

Capped by his country at youth and Under-21 level, Spiegel travelled to the FIFA Under-17 World Cup finals in Nigeria back in 2009 where Switzerland won the tournament for the first time in their history.

Since his arrival in England, he has gained valuable experience with loan spells at Crawley Town, Barnet and Carlisle United before returning to the Hammers and continuing his development under the watchful eye of goalkeeping coach Chris Woods.

The 2015/16 season saw him named on the bench for first-team fixtures and his penalty shootout heroics in the second-leg of the Under-21 Premier League Cup away to Hull City were instrumental in the young Hammers lifting the trophy. With Darren Randolph granted an extended summer break following Euro 2016, Spiegel enjoyed additional pre-season game-time with appearances against Seattle Sounders and Carolina RailHawks during the club's US tour.

Reece **Oxford**

POSITION: Midfielder
DATE OF BIRTH: 16 December 1998
PLACE OF BIRTH: Edmonton

Named as a substitute for the Hammers first-team League Cup tie with Sheffield United in August 2014, aged just 15, Reece Oxford is a phenomenal young talent who enjoyed an incredible 2015/16 season.

After surprisingly being released by Tottenham Hotspur, the young defender, who also has the ability to also operate in holding midfield role, joined the Hammers Academy at U13 level. After continually impressing through the age groups, he made his U18 debut against Norwich City, while still an U15 schoolboy.

He made history at the Boleyn Ground on 2 July 2015 when he made his first-team debut in the UEFA Europa League against FC Lusitans, becoming the club's youngest-ever player - aged 16 years and 198 days.

A memorable Premier League debut followed on the opening weekend of the season, as he played 79 minutes of the Hammers 2-0 victory over Arsenal at the Emirates Stadium. He ended the 2015/16 campaign having made 12 first-team appearances in various competitions and his talent will continue to be nurtured by Slaven Bilic and the West Ham coaching staff as he looks to fulfil his outstanding potential.

35

HAMMER OF THE YEAR 2016 DIMITRI PAYET

It may well have been the final season for Hammers fans at their beloved Boleyn Ground, a venue where everyone justifiably had their own special moment and favourite player. However, the sheer brilliance of performances produced by talented Frenchman Dimitri Payet during that farewell campaign will have certainly added to the list of memorable moments and star performers to strut their stuff in Claret and Blue at the Boleyn.

Payet was signed from Marseille in the summer of 2015 by new boss Slaven Bilic and the little magician wasted no time in showing the Hammers faithful just what he was all about.

His introduction to the Premier League arrived at the Emirates on the opening weekend of the season as he set up Cheikhou Kouyate for the opening goal in the Hammers' 2-0 win at Arsenal. Payet's first Premier League goal arrived against Leicester City and strikes against Newcastle United (two), Sunderland and Crystal Palace followed before injury ruled him out for seven games in November and December.

It was not just Payet's goals and accuracy from set-piece situations that won him so many instant admirers but his ability, awareness and understanding of teammates, that saw him create so many chances for others wearing the West Ham shirt.

He returned from injury to inspire a 2-0 victory over Liverpool before getting back on the scoresheet with a trademark free-kick away to Bournemouth. He then proceeded to crash home that unstoppable free-kick in the FA Cup tie against Manchester United at Old Trafford that will live long in the memory of the travelling masses.

With 12 goals and 15 assists for other goalscorers plus a plethora of exciting opportunities created for teammates during his debut season with the club, his winning of the final Hammer of Year award to be presented at the Boleyn Ground was something of a formality.

Such was the success of his first season with the Hammers, Payet's confidence was clearly sky high as headed back to his homeland in May to link up with his international teammates for the Euro 2016 tournament.

If ever there was a player that a nation needed to see replicate club form for their country then Payet was the man. Suffice to say he did not disappoint. Performing on home soil certainly added to the pressure on Payet and the French team but they, and Payet in particular, got the tournament off to the best possible start.

Placed in Group A with Romania, Albania and Switzerland, France opened the tournament against Romania on 10 June in Paris. Payet was named the man of the match after setting up Olivier Giroud for the opening goal and then in the final minute superbly curling home a left-foot shot for France's second goal in a 2-1 win.

The French left it late again against Albania in their second group match but for the second consecutive game Payet was named the man of the match. He created six scoring chances for his teammates and supplied 17 crosses in a game which the French eventually won 2-0 despite not gaining the breakthrough until the 90th minute. A resolute Albanian defence was eventually broken in the final minute by Antoine Griezmann before Payet added the second deep into injury-time.

The French side played out a 0-0 draw with Switzerland in their final group game and then saw off the Republic of Ireland in Lyon at the round of 16 stage. That 2-1 victory over Darren Randolph's Republic side subsequently teed-up a quarter-final meeting with the tournament's surprise package Iceland in Paris. Payet was once again on the scoresheet as the host nation produced a devastating first-half display to lead 5-0 at the break. Iceland reduced the arrears after the interval as the game finished 5-2 but Payet and France now had a semi-final date with Germany.

Despite overcoming Germany to reach the final, the tournament ended on a frustrating note for the French and particularly for Payet who was substituted in a disappointing final which Portugal eventually won 1-0 after extra time.

After his exploits for the Hammers in 2015/16 and for France in Euro 2016 Payet was given an extended break by Bilic ahead of the new season at London Stadium.

As the Hammers were settling in at their new home, Payet produced another piece of sublime individual skill to score a memorable solo effort against Middlesbrough in October, that already looks like the strike to beat, in the goal of the season stakes.

41

West Ham United were certainly well represented at last summer's Euro 2016 finals in France.

Hammer of the Year Dimitri Payet transferred his sparking club form to country as he inspired the host national all the way to the final in Paris. However, Payet was certainly not the only Hammer to make his mark on the tournament.

EURO 2016 HAMMERS

Darren **Randolph**

REPUBLIC OF IRELAND

Such were the quality of his performances when deputising for Adrian in the West Ham goal during the 2015/16 season, Republic of Ireland manager Martin O'Neill had little hesitation in naming Darren Randolph as his first choice 'keeper at Euro 2016.

Pitched in the tricky Group E along with Sweden, Italy and much-fancied Belgium, Randolph and his teammates were always going to have their work cut out if they were to progress to the knockout stages but it was a challenge they rose to and in dramatic fashion.

The Republic opened their campaign against Sweden and took the lead thanks to a sweetly struck effort from Norwich's Wes Hoolahan. As Zlatan Ibrahimovic and his teammates went in search of an equaliser, Randolph pulled off a string of fine saves to help keep his country in front but he was finally beaten by an unfortunate Ciaran Clark own goal after 71 minutes as the Irish held on for a useful point.

The Boys in Green suffered a 3-0 reversal at the hands of a rampant Belgium in their second fixture which left them needing to beat Italy in their final group game to give them any chance of progressing to the latter stages.

Once again Randolph produced an assured display to keep the Italian side, which included club teammate Angelo Ogbonna, at bay - while at the other end the Norwich City duo of Hoolahan and Robbie Brady combined for Brady to head home a memorable 85th-minute winner to take the Irish through to a last 16 meeting with hosts France.

The France match again saw Randolph come face-to-face with one of his Hammers teammates, this time in the shape of Dimitri Payet. Although Brady converted a second-minute penalty to give them an early lead, it was not to be for Randolph and the Irish as an Antoine Griezmann brace in the second half ended the Republic's progress in the competition.

Having featured in every one of the Republic's four matches and playing a vital role in helping his country proceed from a tough group, Randolph will no doubt reflect proudly on an impressive summer performance.

James **Collins**

WALES

After playing 25 games for the Hammers in all competitions in 2015/16 the ever-popular James Collins headed off to France in the summer with Wales.

Rank outsiders with little in terms of expectation, the Wales team enjoyed a truly outstanding Euro 2016 as they progressed all the way to the semi-finals before bowing out to eventual champions Portugal.

Patience was certainly the key for Collins in France as he was forced to watch on as Wales' boss Chris Coleman opted for a first choice central defensive pairing of Ashley Williams and James Chester.

The Welsh found themselves in Group B alongside England, Russia and Slovakia. They got their campaign off to the best possible start as goals from Gareth Bale and Hal Robson-Kanu gave them a 2-1 victory over Slovakia. Despite surrendering a one-goal lead to lose 2-1 to England in their next match, the Welsh ended up topping group B following a 3-0 demolition of Russia.

The knockout stage saw Wales face Northern Ireland and again Collins watched on from the substitute's bench as a Gareth McAuley own goal saw Coleman's brave dragons through to a quarter-final meeting with Belgium.

Few outside of the principality gave the Welsh team any chance of overcoming the highly impressive Belgians. However, Wales caused the upset of the tournament with a truly memorable 3-1 triumph and Collins finally got to taste tournament football as he replaced Aaron Ramsey in the dying moments of what was Welsh football's finest hour.

Collins was handed a starting role in the semi-final against Portugal as Coleman was forced to shuffle his pack following the suspension of Ramsey. Second-half goals from Cristiano Ronaldo and Nani saw the Welsh fairytale come to an end but Collins and his teammates received a wonderful reception when they returned to Cardiff following what was undoubtedly a major career highlight for all involved.

Angelo **Ogbonna**

Having enjoyed an impressive debut season at the Boleyn Ground following his switch from Juventus in July 2015, commanding central defender Angelo Ogbonna was included in Antonio Conte's Italy squad for Euro 2016.

Ogbonna and his Italian teammates found themselves in Group E with Sweden, Belgium and the Republic of Ireland.

Ogbonna was an unused substitute as Italy won their two opening games against Belgium and Sweden, 2-0 and 1-0 respectively. With progress to the knockout stages as group winners already guaranteed, Conte utilised his squad for the final group match against the Republic of Ireland in Lille on 22 June. Ogbonna was handed his ninth international outing and a place in the back four as he found himself up against West Ham teammate Darren Randolph who was of course in goal for the opposition. In a game the Irish had to win, a late Robbie Brady header sealed a 1-0 victory to give Randolph the bragging rights over Ogbonna when the two reunited for pre-season training.

The Italian's went on to defeat Spain in the round of 16 before exiting the competition after losing an epic penalty shoot-out to Germany at the quarter-final stage.

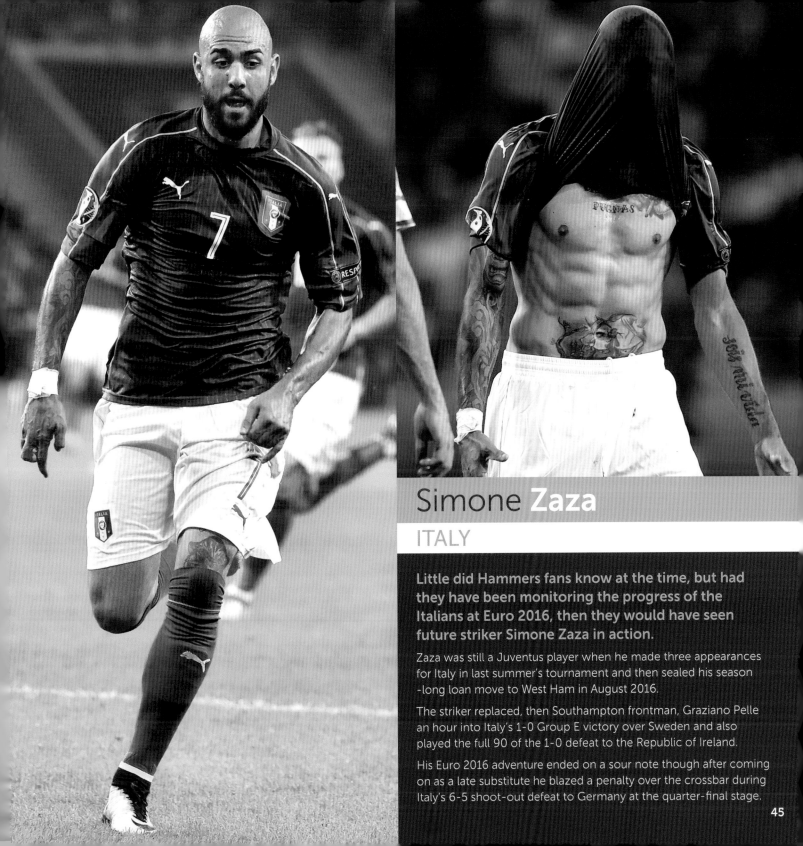

Simone **Zaza**

ITALY

Little did Hammers fans know at the time, but had they have been monitoring the progress of the Italians at Euro 2016, then they would have seen future striker Simone Zaza in action.

Zaza was still a Juventus player when he made three appearances for Italy in last summer's tournament and then sealed his season-long loan move to West Ham in August 2016.

The striker replaced, then Southampton frontman, Graziano Pelle an hour into Italy's 1-0 Group E victory over Sweden and also played the full 90 of the 1-0 defeat to the Republic of Ireland.

His Euro 2016 adventure ended on a sour note though after coming on as a late substitute he blazed a penalty over the crossbar during Italy's 6-5 shoot-out defeat to Germany at the quarter-final stage.

45

CULT heroes

KEN BROWN

A true Hammers hero who enjoyed both FA Cup success and European Cup Winners' Cup glory, Ken Brown made 474 appearances for the club in all competitions between 1953 and 1967.

A committed and reliable defender, Brown was born in Forest Gate, London on 16 February 1934 and was spotted playing for local Dagenham side Neville United, before joining West Ham United in October 1951. He quickly made his mark in the reserve side, but found first-team football much harder to come by, with his West Ham debut eventually coming in February 1953 against Rotherham United. During his first five years as a professional, he only made occasional appearances and national service between 1952 and 1954 hardly helped his cause.

Brown began the 1957/58 season as the first-choice central defender in the heart of the West Ham defence and missed just three games as the Hammers won the Second Division title. On 18 November 1959, Brown won his one and only international cap, helping England secure a 2-1 victory over Northern Ireland at Wembley.

Always fondly remember by Hammers fans who were fortunate to have seen him in action, Brown was a member of the club's 1964 FA Cup winning team and was back at Wembley the following year as part of the European Cup Winners' Cup winning side, playing alongside Bobby Moore. He was also the second-ever recipient of the Hammer of the- Year award, landing the title in 1959.

On Monday 15 May 1967, Brown was given a testimonial match to mark his 14 years distinguished service to the club. As the curtain came down on one remarkable West Ham career, another was just beginning. Brown's testimonial match saw Billy Bonds don a Claret and Blue shirt for the first time.

Brown ended his Football League playing career with a spell at Torquay United alongside his former West Ham United teammate John Bond. He subsequently coached for Bond at Bournemouth and Norwich before taking the reins at Carrow Road and masterminding two promotions to the top flight and League Cup success for the Canaries at Wembley in 1985.

His son Kenny Brown (Jnr) also went on to play for West Ham between 1991 and 1996. In February 2004, Brown was a guest of honour at Carrow Road for the Canaries' match with West Ham to celebrate the opening of a new South Stand and a special presentation was made to commemorate his 70th birthday. He remains an ever-popular character whenever attending a Hammers fixture.

2015/16 SEASON REVIEW

The 2015/16 season was always going to be a special one for West Ham United as the club completed its final season at the Boleyn Ground. New boss Slaven Bilic and his players certainly made sure the old ground was given a great send off with a memorable campaign as the Hammers entertained throughout and enjoyed an exciting FA Cup run and a seventh place finish in the Premier League.

After ending the previous campaign top of the Premier League fair play table, the Hammers were rewarded with a place in the qualifying stages of the 2015/16 Europa League. This resulted in an early return to competitive action and Bilic's Boleyn Ground return got off to the best possible start when he was introduced to a full house prior for the first leg of a first qualifying round match with Andorran side Lusitans. Academy manager Terry Westley took charge and Bilic looked on as goals from Diafra Sakho (two) and James Tomkins sealed a comfortable 3-0 win.

A 1-0 victory in the second leg in Andorra set up a second qualifying round match with Maltese side Birkirkara before the Hammers sadly bowed out of the competition at the third qualifying round stage after suffering a 4-3 aggregate defeat to Romanian outfit Astra Giurgiu. Exiting Europe was a disappointment but the early return to competitive matches certainly ensured the Hammers were firing on all cylinders and hit the ground running when the new Premier League season got underway.

A tough opening fixture away to Arsenal was conquered in style as Bilic marked his first game as a Premier League manager by masterminding an impressive 2-0 victory at the Emirates. The busy opening month of August saw back-to-back home defeats to Leicester City and newly-promoted Bournemouth but ended with a historic 3-0 victory over Liverpool at Anfield.

It was a case of third time lucky for the Hammers on home soil as September began with a comprehensive 2-0 triumph over Newcastle United at the Boleyn. A highly impressive 2-1 win away to Manchester City was followed by an early League Cup exit at the hands of Leicester and a 2-2 draw at home to Norwich City as September's fixtures came to a close and left the club sitting proudly third in the Premier League table.

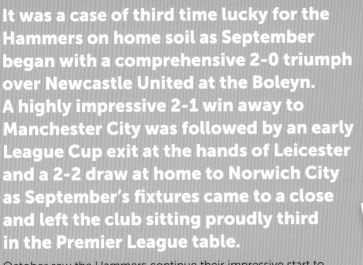

October saw the Hammers continue their impressive start to the campaign with seven points from four games. London derby triumphs away to Crystal Palace and at home to Chelsea were sandwiched in between a 2-2 draw at Sunderland and a surprise 2-0 defeat at Watford.

A spell of two months without a Premier League victory saw Bilic's troops slip from third in the table, after defeating Chelsea on 24 October, to tenth prior to the 2-1 win at home to Southampton on 28 December. However, during that seven-match spell the team only suffered one defeat, a 4-1 reversal to a rampant Spurs at White Hart Lane. The other six games ended all-square and included hard fought points from trips to Manchester United and Swansea. The calendar year of 2015 ended on a winning note as Andy Carroll came off the bench to head home the winner against Southampton to secure a 2-1 win at the Boleyn and hoist the Hammers up to seventh in the table.

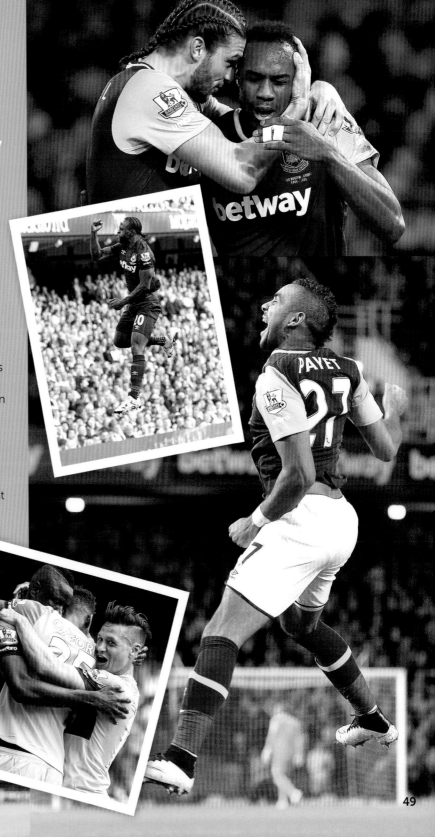

2015/16 SEASON REVIEW

The new year began in the best possible way as star man Dimitri Payet marked his return from injury by inspiring a 2-0 home success against Liverpool that gave the Hammers a rare league double over the Merseysiders. Next on the agenda was the club's pursuit of FA Cup glory which began with a 1-0 victory at home to Wolves in the third round. A midweek triumph over Bournemouth was made particularly memorable due to an exquisite free-kick from Payet during a 3-1 triumph before the January league programme was completed with a narrow defeat at Newcastle and an entertaining 2-2 draw at home to Manchester City.

Reward for defeating Wolves in the FA Cup was a testing fourth round trip to Liverpool. However, Bilic's men once again showed their metal to force a replay on home soil after a goalless draw at Anfield on 30 January. A 2-0 victory over struggling Aston Villa at the Boleyn was followed by a 1-0 defeat at Southampton ahead of the eagerly-awaited cup replay against the Reds. A passionate cup-tie played under the lights unfolded and a penalty shoot-out looked on the cards until Angelo Ogbonna picked the perfect time to head home his first goal in claret and blue to seal a memorable 2-1 extra-time triumph and a fifth round trip to Blackburn Rovers.

February continued to be a positive month in terms of collecting Premier League points as the Hammers battled back from 2-0 down at Carrow Road to salvage a point against Norwich City. A 1-0 win at home to Sunderland came on the back of the highly impressive 5-1 demolition of Blackburn Rovers at Ewood Park in the fifth round of the FA Cup that in turn set up a quarter-final meeting with Manchester United at Old Trafford.

March got off to a flying start as the Hammers avenged their 4-1 defeat at White Hart Lane with a 1-0 triumph over title-chasing Spurs at the Boleyn on 2 March. That win was swiftly followed by a 3-2 victory over Everton at Goodison Park as Bilic's troops found themselves sitting fifth in the Premier League table as they headed straight back to the north west to take on Manchester United in the FA Cup. Once again a beautifully executed free-kick from Payet lit up the match and looked to have booked the Hammers a semi-final slot until the hosts hit back with an Anthony Martial equaliser seven minutes from time to force a replay.

A hat-trick of London derbies ended all-square before the quarter-final replay as the team recorded 2-2 draws away to Chelsea and at home to Crystal Palace before an Andy Carroll treble secured a 3-3 draw at home to Arsenal. With the FA Cup semi-finals scheduled for Wembley, the quarter-final replay against Manchester United was guaranteed to be the very last FA Cup tie played at the Boleyn Ground. Sadly it was not to end on a happy note as goals from Marcus Rashford and Marouane Fellaini fired the visitors into the semi-finals despite a late West Ham flurry.

Despite the gut wrenching cup exit, the Hammers dusted themselves down to secure a point away to champions elect Leicester City before ending the month of April with comprehensive victories over Watford and West Bromwich Albion.

The final month of the season saw two contrasting matches at the Boleyn and a final day trip to Stoke City. The 4-1 defeat suffered at home to Swansea City on 7 May would have been an awful way to end life at the Boleyn but fortunately three days later it all came right on the final night. With Manchester United the visitors, the match offered precious Premier League points and revenge for the FA Cup defeat the previous month. A pulsating affair ended with Winston Reid scoring the final goal at the old ground as the Hammers ran out 3-2 winners. The campaign ended with a 2-1 defeat away to Stoke City and a seventh placed finish which in turn resulted in qualification for the qualifying rounds of the Europa League once again in 2016/17.

MARK NOBLE'S TESTIMONIAL MATCH

West Ham United XI 6
West Ham United All-stars 5

WEST HAM XI: Adrian (Spiegel 29, Hatton 76), O'Brien, Tomkins (Pike 46), Reid (A Ferdinand 65, Dobson 85), Cresswell (Dobson 58, Collins 81), Song (Short 76), Obiang (Noble 65), Noble (Browne 46), Lanzini (Di Canio 65), Antonio (Sinclair 65), Emenike (Sakho 22, Diangana 58, Carroll 81).

WEST HAM ALL-STARS (First-half): James, Ward (Dailly 15), R Ferdinand, A Ferdinand, Dicks (Gabbidon 15), Downing (Sinclair 15), Collison, Parker (Di Canio 15), Benayoun, Bellamy, C Cole.

(Second-half): Walker (Miklosko 81), Lomas (Powell 58), Dailly, Upson (Blewitt 65), Gabbidon (Keen 65), Bowyer (Cohen 77), Collison (Moncur 51, Bishop 65), Harewood, Etherington, Sheringham, Ashton (Tombides 77).

Despite engineering works resulting in no tube service running to the Boleyn Ground - an amazing 35,036 Hammers fans turned up to salute long-serving captain Mark Noble's commitment to the club when his testimonial match look place on Monday 28 March 2016.

The fixture saw a West Ham Xl take on a team of Hammers all-stars in what was not only a celebration of Noble's career but also a wonderful opportunity to see a host of club legends return to the Boleyn Ground during the famous old ground's farewell season.

All who overcame the travel obstacles for this Bank Holiday fixture were treated to a trip down memory lane as faces new and old took to the field. Noble, celebrating 12 years in West Ham's first team, entered from the tunnel and walked through a guard of honour - flanked by his young children Honey and Lenny - made up of his current and former teammates, standing either side in West Ham's home and away colours.

Once the game got underway, it took less than three minutes before a rendition of 'Stand up, if you love West Ham' began and the whole stadium rose to its feet. Then when Paolo Di Canio entered the fray on 16 minutes the 'Paolo Di Canio' wave of noise accompanied him.

An afternoon packed with memorable moments including a goal from Noble plus an outstanding overhead kick from Dean Ashton will live long in the memory for all who were fortunate enough to witness this wonderful event.

The fact that so many former West Ham greats returned to participate in the match clearly demonstrated that the respect for Noble among his playing peers is equally matched with the affection that he receives from the club's supporters.

Congratulations Mark!

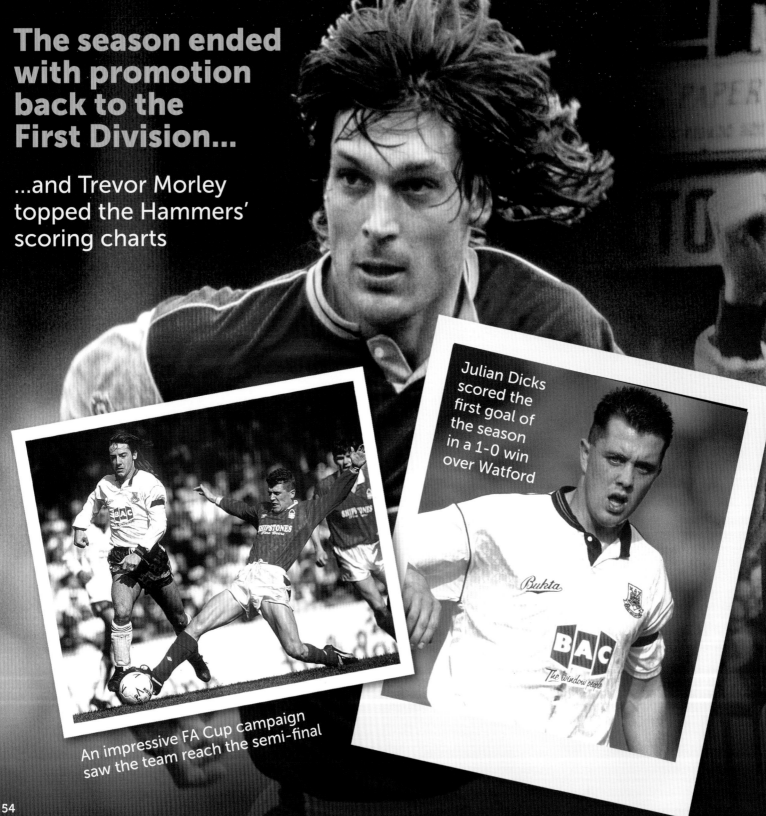

The season ended with promotion back to the First Division...

...and Trevor Morley topped the Hammers' scoring charts

Julian Dicks scored the first goal of the season in a 1-0 win over Watford

An impressive FA Cup campaign saw the team reach the semi-final

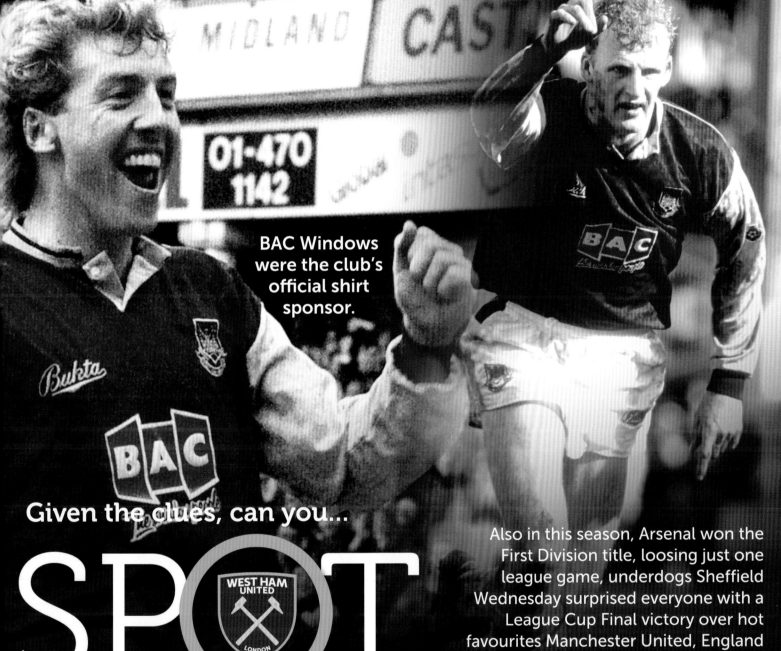

BAC Windows were the club's official shirt sponsor.

Given the clues, can you...

SPOT THE SEASON

WEST HAM UNITED
LONDON

ANSWER ON PAGE 82

Also in this season, Arsenal won the First Division title, loosing just one league game, underdogs Sheffield Wednesday surprised everyone with a League Cup Final victory over hot favourites Manchester United, England beat Hungary 1-0 in Graham Taylor's first game as manager,

...and the Hammers beat Hull City 7-1 in the biggest Second Division win of the season.

2015/16 QUIZ OF THE YEAR

The 2015/16 season was a historic campaign for the Hammers who bade farewell to the Boleyn Ground - the club's iconic home for 112 years.

So what can you recall of matters on the pitch from last season? Here's 20 for you to tackle...

1

From which club did the Hammers sign Angelo Ogbonna in July 2015?

6

West Ham enjoyed a rare victory over Liverpool at Anfield in August 2015 - who played in goal for the Hammers and kept a clean sheet?

2

Against which side did Slaven Bilic suffer his first Premier League defeat as West Ham manager?

4

How many goals in total did the Hammers score in their 2015/16 Europa League campaign?

7

Who scored West Ham's opening goal to set them on their way to victory away to Manchester City?

9

Two players netted hat-tricks at the Boleyn Ground last season - can you name them both?

3

Winger Matt Jarvis left West Ham to join which Championship side (initially on loan) in the summer transfer window?

5

Can you name the club that knocked the Hammers out of the League Cup in September 2015?

8

Which Championship club were West Ham paired with in the FA Cup third round ?

10

Which Hammers legend was rewarded with a testimonial match at the Boleyn Ground in March 2016?

11

Can you name the one club that the Hammers completed a Premier League double over in 2015/16?

13

From which club did Sam Byram join the Hammers in the January transfer window?

16

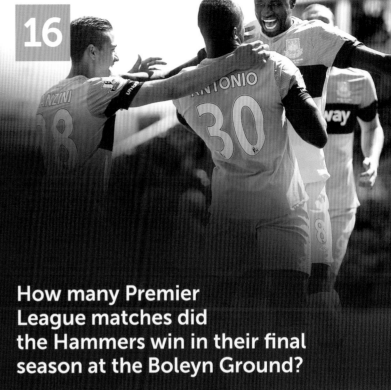

How many Premier League matches did the Hammers win in their final season at the Boleyn Ground?

12

Who scored the Hammers' first goal in the calendar year of 2016?

14

The Hammers scored ten goals in their 2015/16 FA Cup run, can you name the top scorer and how many goals he scored?

15

Captain Mark Noble was the Hammers most cautioned player in the Premier League last season.
How many yellow cards was he shown during the league campaign?

17

Can you recall the total number of Premier League goals the Hammers scored last season? Was it more than 66, less than 66 or 66 exactly?

19

In all competitions last season, the Hammers scored more goals away, than at home. True or false?

18

Who was runner-up in last season's 'Hammer of the Year' voting?

20

Can you name the player who took the mantle of scoring the club's last-ever goal at the Boleyn Ground?

West Ham United have been blessed with some truly great goalscorers over the years and also with a host of players who have netted score memorable goals, but will there ever be a pairing to better the phenomenal achievements of Frank McAvennie and Tony Cottee?

DOUBLE
McAVENNIE

Both Cottee and McAvennie were quality strikers in their own right, but John Lyall's decision to bring the pair together was a masterstroke that almost resulted in the Hammers lifting the First Division title in 1985/86.

Cottee, born in Forest Gate on 11 July 1965, began his career with West Ham and proved to be a consistent goalscorer at both youth and reserve team level. It was of little surprise that he was handed his first-team debut at the age of just 17 and unsurprisingly, he marked the occasion with a goal as the Hammers registered a 3-0 New Year's Day victory over Spurs at the Boleyn Ground in 1983.

McAvennie meanwhile, had carved out a growing reputation for himself by scoring 48 league goals from 135 outings for St Mirren in his native Scotland. He was born in Glasgow on 22 November 1959 and his goalscoring exploits at Love Street brought his talents to the attention of a number of English clubs. Despite strong interest from Luton Town in the summer of 1985, McAvennie eventually joined West Ham and arrived at the Boleyn Ground for a reported fee of £340,000.

His debut came on the opening day of 1985/86 as the Hammers slipped to a narrow 1-0 defeat away to Birmingham City.

McAvennie marked his home debut by bagging a brace in a 3-1 victory over Queens Park Rangers, while playing alongside Cottee. It was the beginning of a successful partnership and a memorable campaign for the club.

ACTS
& COTTEE

The Cottee/McAvennie double-act went on to yield an incredible 46 league goals during the 1985/86 season as the Hammers stood toe-to-toe with Merseyside giants Liverpool and Everton in a three-way race for the title. Sadly Lyall's men fell four points short of top slot and ended a truly memorable campaign in third place - the club's best-ever top-flight finish.

McAvennie weighed in with 26 league goals, while strike partner Cottee registered 20 and it was the local hero Cottee who won the 1986 Hammer of the Year accolade, with his sidekick as runner-up.

In October 1987 McAvennie joined Celtic, but returned to the Boleyn Ground for a second spell at the club - in total he played 190 games for West Ham scoring 60 goals. Ironically Cottee also returned to West Ham for a second spell after leaving the club for Everton in August 1988 - he played in a total of 336 games for the Hammers across his two spells and scored 146 goals.

UNDER 23 SQUAD 16/17

Luka **Belic**

A Serbian U19 international, Luka Belic joined the Hammers from OFK Beograd in September 2015 and made an impressive contribution to the U21 squad's 2015/16 season.

The young striker became the youngest player to feature in the Serbian top flight, aged 16 in 2012. He played his first Hammers match against Newcastle United U21s and created a goal in a 2-2 draw. His first West Ham goal came against Derby U21s on 1 February during a season that saw the Hammers seal a seventh-place finish in the U21 Premier League table.

Marcus **Browne**

Midfielder Marcus Browne joined the Hammers Academy at the age of eight and after overcoming a difficult spell with injuries in 2013/14 has become an integral part of the development squad.

Last season proved a real breakthrough campaign for Browne who continued to star on a regular basis for the U21 side, before savouring first-team involvement in the early part of 2016. His form earned him a place on the bench for the senior squad's trip to Norwich City in the Premier League on 13 February and he was also a substitute against Blackburn Rovers in the FA Cup game a week later.

Browne also played a major part in both legs of the Premier League U21 Cup Final against Hull City when West Ham got their hands on the trophy following a tense penalty shootout.

Josh Cullen

The 2015/16 season certainly proved to be a momentous campaign for all-action central midfield Josh Cullen. Born in Southend-on-Sea, Cullen progressed though the U18 and development squad sides to make three appearances for the first team in their early season UEFA Europa League qualifiers.

As captain of the U21 development side, Cullen continued to remain involved with the first-team and made his Premier League bow as a substitute in the 3-0 victory over Liverpool and was also an unused substitute for a number of first-team games during December. In January 2016, he joined League One Bradford City on loan and helped the Bantams reach the end-of-season Play-Offs. Such was the impression he made at Valley Parade, he has since re-joined Bradford for a second loan spell, agreeing a five-month loan in August 2016.

Grady Diangana

Creative midfielder Grady Diangana initially joined the Hammers at the age of 12. Originally a striker, he was converted to an attacking midfielder when playing at U15 level.

After making 24 appearances for the U18 side in 2014/15, when his performances proved to be a thorn in the side of several opposing defences, he stepped up to play regularly for the U21 side last season and will be keen to show what he can do at U23 level over the coming months of the 2016/17 campaign.

Reece Burke

A tall, determined and accomplished defender capable of playing at either centre-back or right-back, Reece Burke joined the West Ham United Academy at the age of nine and has progressed to play for the first-team.

His full debut came in the FA Cup third round defeat at Nottingham Forest on 5 January 2014 and he has since progressed to make League Cup and Premier League appearances for the club at first-team level. After spending the 2015/16 campaign on loan at League One Bradford City where he helped the Bantams progress to the League One Play-Offs, Burke will be plying his trade at Championship level in 2016/17, after agreeing a season-long loan with Gary Caldwell's Wigan Athletic.

George Dobson

Midfielder George Dobson joined his boyhood club West Ham United from London rivals Arsenal in July 2015 and enjoyed an impressive debut season with Terry Westley's U21 squad during the 2015/16 campaign.

A key member of the U21 team's midfield as they climbed the table and targeted the play-off spots, Dobson was named on the first-team substitutes' bench for March matches against Spurs and Everton and featured in the first-leg of the U21 Premier League Cup final against Hull City. The young midfielder is currently gaining valuable experience on loan with League One side Walsall.

Sam Ford

Striker Sam Ford began his career playing in the Ipswich Town Academy before joining the Hammers in March 2016.

The lively forward scored his first goal in Claret and Blue just 12 minutes into his debut for the U21 side against Wolverhampton Wanderers. As the season progressed, Ford was part of the development squad which reached the final and lifted the 2016 U21 Premier League Cup against Hull City. Ford will be keen to continue his development and look to impress all at the club in 2016/17.

Jaanai Gordon

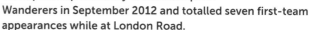

Jaanai Gordon came through the ranks at Peterborough United and signed his first professional contract with Posh on his 17th birthday in December 2012. He made his first-team debut for Peterborough in a 2-0 home Championship defeat by Wolverhampton Wanderers in September 2012 and totalled seven first-team appearances while at London Road.

After a trial spell with the Hammers, he joined West Ham United on 1 January 2014 and was an unused substitute for the FA Cup third round defeat at Nottingham Forest later that month. Mixed among outings for the U21 side, Gordon has also taken in loan spells with non-league sides Chelmsford City and Nuneaton Town, before joining League of Ireland side Sligo Rovers on loan in March 2016.

Sam Howes

Goalkeeper Sam Howes joined West Ham United at U10 level from Crystal Palace and progressed through the Academy ranks to make his U18 Premier League debut by starting at Blackburn Rovers on 1 December 2012.

He capped a superb 2013/14 season by winning the Young Hammer of the Year award and joined the first-team squad on their Football United Tour of New Zealand in July 2014. His first-team debut arrived during the Football United Tour fixture with Sydney FC in July 2014. Capped by England at a host of youth levels, Howes flitted between the Hammers U18 and U21s during the 2015/16 season and will be looking to cement his place at U23 level this season.

Kyle Knoyle

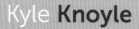

England U18 international full-back Kyle Knoyle initially joined the West Ham United Academy as a 13-year-old after being recommended by coaches on a Junior Hammers coaching course. His progress though the ranks resulted in a two-year professional contract in 2015.

An attacking full-back who loves to get forward and support the attack, Knoyle played a part in the Club's UEFA Europa League qualifiers in 2015/16 before joining Scottish Premiership side Dundee United on loan in January. He helped the Tannadice club reach the semi-finals of the Scottish Cup, before losing to Hibernian on penalties. Along with teammate Reece Burke, Knoyle has joined Championship club Wigan Athletic on loan for the 2016/17 season.

UNDER 23 SQUAD 16/17

Moses Makasi

Defensive midfielder Moses Makasi signed his first professional contract with West Ham United in the summer of 2014 after an impressive two-year scholarship at the club's Academy.

Makasi, who is strong in the tackle and composed in possession, played a key part in the U21 side's league campaign in 2015/16. He also scored in the 4-0 away Premier League Cup win against Exeter City on 2 December at St. James' Park and netted again on 11 March against Newcastle - at the country's other St. James' Park. Makasi also had a major influence in helping Terry Westley's men win the Premier League U21 Cup after a two-legged victory over Hull City.

Toni Martinez

West Ham United completed the signing of 18-year-old Spanish striker Toni Martinez from Valencia in April 2016. The teenage goalscoring sensation was a prolific marksman for Valencia's youth teams and agreed a three-year contract with the Hammers.

His goalscoring exploits in his homeland gained international recognition from Spain at U17 level and his progress with the Hammers over the coming weeks and months is sure to be keenly monitored by both club and country.

Vashon Neufville

An England U16 international defender, Vashon Neufville spent time with Chelsea before joining the West Ham United Academy as an U14. He made his U18 Premier League debut in a goalless home draw with Leicester City on 23 August 2014.

During 2015/16, he made 14 appearances for the U18s during the course of the season. He also played eight times for Terry Westley's U21 team and has sine signed a new long-term deal with the club.

Lewis Page

Attack-minded left-back Lewis Page signed his first professional contract with the club in the summer of 2014. During the 2014/15 season, he established himself in the development squad where his fantastic range of passing, energy and desire won him many admirers.

The defender started both games against Lusitanos in the UEFA Europa League and the away leg against Astra before his U21 form was rewarded with a loan spell at League Two side Cambridge United. His Football League debut came against AFC Wimbledon on 2 January. Page played six times for the club before returning to Rush Green to play a part in the U21s' Premier League Cup victory. Further league experience will come the youngster's way with a loan spell agreed with League One Coventry City for the first-half of the 2016/17 season.

Djair **Parfitt-Williams**

Djair Parfitt-Williams is an exciting forward with the ability to operate as an out-and-out striker, a winger on either flank or in the creative number 10 role. This Bermuda-born, United States-raised forward was spotted by West Ham United legend Clyde Best as part of the Hammers' international scouting programme when he was playing for San Jose Earthquakes in the USA.

He represented the U18 side when still a schoolboy and was top scorer at that level in 2014/15. Last season he stepped up to the U21 development squad and made his first-team debut as a substitute in the UEFA Europa League match against Lusitanos. His great form for the development squad, was rewarded with a place on the first-team bench for Premier League fixtures against Norwich and Liverpool.

Josh **Pask**

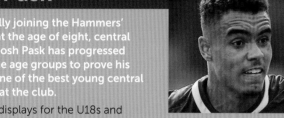

After initially joining the Hammers' Academy at the age of eight, central defender Josh Pask has progressed through the age groups to prove his worth as one of the best young central defenders at the club.

Confident displays for the U18s and the development squad side saw his reputation grow and he was named on the first-team bench against Astra in the UEFA Europa League tie at the start of the 2015/16 campaign. Pask then joined League Two outfit Dagenham and Redbridge on loan in October and made his debut Football League against Hartlepool United on 17 October 2015. The young defender will continue his development with a season-long loan with League One Gillingham in 2016/17.

Alex **Pike**

Defender Alex Pike joined West Ham United as an U11 midfielder before being converted to a right-back as a schoolboy. After progressing through the Academy age groups, Pike made his U18 Premier League debut while still an U16 schoolboy at home to Tottenham Hotspur back in January 2013.

He featured 13 times for the U18s in the league in 2013/14, having missed the opening half of the season with a knee injury. After standout performances in 2014/15 at U18 and U21 level, Pike made a first-team substitute appearance against Astra in the UEFA Europa League in early August. Last season he played a key role as Terry Westley's men reached the U21 Premier League Cup Final against Hull City, which they won on penalties at the KC Stadium.

64

Declan **Rice**

With the ability to operate as either a holding midfielder or central defender, Declan Rice joined the Hammers Academy at U14 level, having previously been with Chelsea.

The young Irishman is highly rated among the coaching staff at the Academy and enjoyed an excellent 2015/16 season with both the U18 and U21 sides. Part of the development squad's Premier League Cup success, Rice completed a fantastic campaign by winning the Dylan Tombides Award in recognition of his performances for the Academy at the end of the season.

Noha **Sylvestre**

Central midfielder Noha Sylvestre joined the Hammers in 2014 from his native Switzerland. He began his career with FC Bure in his homeland, before joining US Boncourt and then Swiss Second Division club FC Concordia Basel as an U16.

Sylvestre made his debut for U18s on the opening day of the season with a convincing 3-1 win over West Bromwich Albion and became a consistent performer for the U18 team during the 2014/15 campaign. Last season, he played regularly U18 level and also stepped up to make three appearances for the development squad. The Swiss U17 international will look to make his mark at U23 level this season.

Nathan **Trott**

Promising Bermudan goalkeeper Nathan Trott joined the Hammers in January 2016 on a two-and-a-half-year deal, following a successful trial period at the club.

Trott, who names Thibaut Courtois, Petr Cech and David De Gea as his goalkeeping heroes, travelled with the development squad to the Netherlands during the 2016/17 pre-season programme. After starting the U23's first two league games of the season, he will be keen to impress at this level during the 2016/17 campaign.

Martin **Samuelsen**

Born in the Norwegian town of Haugesund in April 1997, Martin Samuelsen began his career with local club Vard Haugesund as a schoolboy, where his performances attracted the attention of some of Europe's top clubs. He moved to English football with Manchester City in 2010 at the age of 15 and became a regular in their development squad, while still an Academy scholar.

Following a successful trial with the Hammers, Samuelsen agreed a two-year contract in June 2015. He made his first-team debut in the UEFA Europa League second qualifying round first-leg win over Birkirkara FC of Malta on 16 July 2015. During the 2015/16 season, the young Norwegian played regularly for the development squad, before enjoying a loan spell with League One side Peterborough United. Samuelsen will continue his development during the 2016/17 campaign in the Championship, with a season-long loan at Blackburn Rovers.

Sam **Westley**

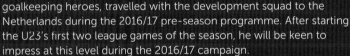

Young defender Sam Westley has the ability to operate in either full-back birth and will be looking to make his mark with the Hammers in 2016/17 after spending last season on loan at Dutch side VVV-Venlo.

Westley began his career as a schoolboy with Birmingham City, before moving to Stoke City where he was a member of the Potters' development squad between 2012 and 2014. He then spent a brief period with Ipswich Town before linking up with the Hammers in July 2014.

The son of Academy Director Terry Westley, Sam enjoyed an impressive first season with the club in 2014/15, starting 13 of the Hammers Barclays Under-21 Premier League fixtures.

At the start of the 2015/16 campaign he was named as an unused substitute for both legs of the Europa League first qualifying round with Andorran side Lusitanos, before sealing his season long loan in Holland.

CULT heroes

MARTIN PETERS

England World Cup-winner and West Ham United legend Martin Peters began his trophy-laden career at the Boleyn Ground and went on to play 364 games for the club and net a century of goals in Claret and Blue.

The son of a Thames lighterman, Peters was born in West Ham territory at Plaistow, in the East End of London, on November, 1943. The family subsequently moved to Dagenham, but Peters joined the Hammers as an apprentice in 1959, and made his senior debut in 1962 in the same side as John Bond and Ken Brown - both of which he would link up with later in his career at Carrow Road.

He missed out on the Hammers' 1964 FA Cup Final success over Preston, but was firmly established in the side when West Ham returned to Wembley a year later to lift the European Cup Winners' Cup, beating TSV Munich 2-0. Peters won 67 full England caps, scoring in the 4-2 World Cup Final victory over West Germany in 1966, in only his eighth game for his country.

In March 1970, Peters became Britain's most expensive player when he joined Spurs for a breathtaking £200,000. While at White Hart Lane he helped Spurs win the League Cup twice and the UEFA Cup in 1972. When Terry Neill replaced Bill Nicholson at the start of the 1974/75 season, his decision to part with 31-year-old Peters soon looked ill-judged. The World Cup-winner joined Norwich City and scored 50 goals in 232 games for the Canaries between 1975 and 1980. The midfield star continued to ooze enthusiasm, dedication, and pure creative class during his five-year Indian summer at Carrow Road.

Peters left Norwich in August 1980 to join Third Division Sheffield United as player-coach and subsequently manager for a short spell.

For both club and country, Peters was famed for his ability to 'ghost' into goalscoring positions on the blind side of defenders. Known as 'the complete midfielder, John Bond claimed that he was virtually impossible to mark and England manager, Sir Alf Ramsey famously described him as 'ten years ahead of his time'.

Can you find eight Premier League managers hidden in the crowd? ANSWERS ON PAGE 82.

FAN'tastic

ACADEMY U18 SQUAD 16/17

Tunji Akinola

Defender Tunji Akinola played his first game for the Hammers' U18 side while still an U15 schoolboy and his maturity helped him become a regular member of the U18 squad when still just 15-years-old.

Akinola began his scholarship at the start of the 2015/16 campaign and started the season playing regularly for the U18 side before progressing to feature for the U21 development squad. He ended a successful season by signing a new long-term deal with the club.

Mason Barrett

First-year scholar Mason Barrett is a versatile defender who has progressed through the various age groups within the Academy set-up at West Ham.

With the ability to operate anywhere across the back four, his flexibility is sure to be a real asset for the U18 team over the 2016/17 season. He begins his first season as a scholar, having been briefly involved with the U18s in 2015/16.

Conor Coventry

Highly-rated box-to-box midfielder Conor Coventry began his scholarship with the Hammers in the summer of 2016. Along with teammate Alfie Lewis, Coventry has also represented the club's U21 side while still at school.

An intelligent player with great awareness of those around him, he has won international recognition with Ireland at U16 level and is expected to make great progress over the coming season.

Jake Eggleton

A fast, attacking right-back who loves to use his pace to help support the attack, Jake Eggleton was a key player for the U16 side in 2014/15 and began his scholarship with the club in the summer of 2015.

Eggleton was one of the youngest players to play for the U18s in 2015/16 and will be hopeful to show his worth for the development squad in 2016/17, while also continuing to study for his A levels.

Malyk Hamilton

Attacking midfielder Malyk Hamilton started his scholarship with the Hammers' Academy in the summer of 2016.

The Canadian began his youth career with Calgary Foothills up until U12 level when he made the switch to West Ham. He was ever-present for the U16 side in 2015/16 and managed a few outings for the U18s while still a schoolboy.

Jahmal Hector-Ingram

Jahmal Hector-Ingram has been part of the Hammers' Academy since he was eight-years-old. The free-scoring striker has also won international recognition with England at youth level.

During 2015/16, Hector-Ingram displayed enormous promise throughout a successful campaign for both the U18s and the development squad. From February onwards, he was regularly selected for the Under 21s and scored against Aston Villa in the final league match of the season.

Korrey Henry

A tall and powerfully-built striker, Korrey Henry was one of the leading scorers for the U16 side last season despite missing parts of the campaign with injury.

He began his scholarship in the summer of 2016 and will be keen to be among the goals on a regular basis for the U18 side during the 2016/17 campaign.

Ben Johnson

Ben Johnson is a pacy winger who clearly loves to excite with his skilful wing play. However, he is not just a provider of opportunities for others, as he demonstrated for the U16 side last season, chipping in with an impressive eight goals.

A first-year scholar, Johnson already has experience of football at U17 and U20 level, having been involved with the squads that travelled to Holland and Switzerland respectively last season.

Dan **Kemp**

Talented winger Dan Kemp began his schoolboy career with Chelsea as a six-year-old, but joined the Hammers in November 2015 on a one-year scholarship.

He played a mixture of U18s and U21s football in his first season with West Ham and showed an eye for goal by scoring in four consecutive fixtures for the U18s against Aston Villa, Southampton, Swansea and Brighton. Kemp was also on target for the development side in a 4-1 win at Newcastle. In May 2016, he agreed a three-year professional contract with the Hammers.

Alfie **Lewis**

An intelligent midfielder player with an impressing range of passing skills, Alfie Lewis is one of a small crop of youngsters who has incredibly, made his debut for the Hammers' U21 side while still a schoolboy.

Lewis is expected to be a main source of creativity and attacking flair for the U18s in 2016/17. Should he continue to show the level of maturity and consistency that he has demonstrated so far in his fledgling career, then he may well progress to the development squad this season too.

Rosaire Longelo

A highly-skilful winger with pace to burn, Rosaire Longelo is another youngster who had progressed though the club's Academy set-up over a number of age groups.

Longelo began his scholarship in the summer of 2016 and his brother, Emmanuel, is part of the U16 squad for the 2016/17 campaign.

Rihards Matrevics

Giant Latvian goalkeeper Rihards Matrevics stands at 6'7 and is certainly an imposing figure for any opposition striker bearing down on goal.

Capped by Latvia's national side at U17 level, Matrevics joined the Hammers' Academy in September 2015 following a successful trial period with the club.

Joe Powell

Pacey winger Joe Powell has produced a number of eye-catching performances for both the U18 and U21 sides. With the ability to change a game at will, he certainly appears to have a great future ahead of him.

The 2015/16 season saw him play 15 times for the U18s during an exciting campaign. He also made a number of appearances for the development squad and ended the season by signing a professional contract with the Hammers.

Anthony Scully

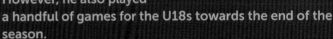

Billed as one of the most exciting players at the Academy, midfielder Anthony Scully played predominantly for the U16s in 2014/15. However, he also played a handful of games for the U18s towards the end of the season.

He began his scholarship with the Hammers last season and played for the U18s, before making his first appearances for the development squad on 14 December against Arsenal at the Boleyn Ground. Scully signed a new deal with the Hammers at the end of the 2015/16 campaign.

Ben Wells

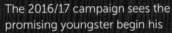

Ben Wells predominately operates in the left-back role, but he remains a versatile defender who can also feature at centre-back or as a defensive midfielder.

The 2016/17 campaign sees the promising youngster begin his scholarship with the Hammers having previously gained great experience by travelling to the Hazza Bin Zayed U17 Cup in early 2015, while still a member of the U16 squad.

ACADEMY U18 SQUAD 16/17

The Hammers' central-defensive partnership of Bobby Moore and Ken Brown in the early 1960s is arguably the yardstick that all West Ham United central-defenders with be judged by.

DOUBLE

GALE &

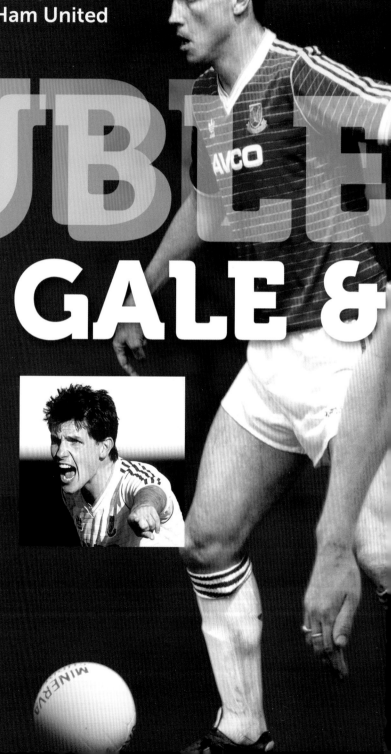

After all, Moore and Brown's marshalling of the opposition's forwards did happen to coincided with FA Cup and European Cup Winners' Cup success! However, another top quality defensive partnership was that of Alvin Martin and Tony Gale who formed the bedrock of the famous 'Boys of 86' side.

Born in Walton, Liverpool on 29 July 1958, Martin was on the books as a schoolboy player at Everton, but failed to agree terms on an apprenticeship deal with the Goodison Park club. An unsuccessful trial with Queens Park Rangers was followed the next day by a successful one at West Ham and Martin signed an apprenticeship contract in August 1974. It was certainly a case of Everton and QPR's loss being the Hammers' gain, as Martin went on to have a highly successful 21-year West Ham career.

Gale had already played over 250 league games for Fulham when he stepped up to the First Division with a £200,000 switch across London to join the Hammers in July 1984. Born in Westminster on 19 November 1959, Gale had been a one club man prior to arriving at the Boleyn Ground after progressing through the ranks at Craven Cottage.

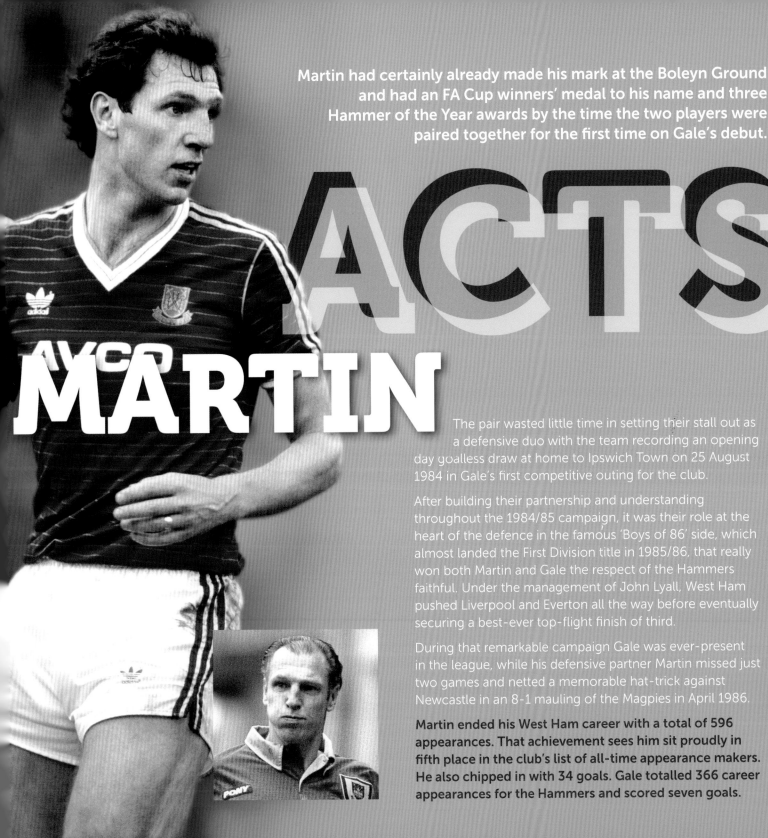

Martin had certainly already made his mark at the Boleyn Ground and had an FA Cup winners' medal to his name and three Hammer of the Year awards by the time the two players were paired together for the first time on Gale's debut.

FACTS

MARTIN

The pair wasted little time in setting their stall out as a defensive duo with the team recording an opening day goalless draw at home to Ipswich Town on 25 August 1984 in Gale's first competitive outing for the club.

After building their partnership and understanding throughout the 1984/85 campaign, it was their role at the heart of the defence in the famous 'Boys of 86' side, which almost landed the First Division title in 1985/86, that really won both Martin and Gale the respect of the Hammers faithful. Under the management of John Lyall, West Ham pushed Liverpool and Everton all the way before eventually securing a best-ever top-flight finish of third.

During that remarkable campaign Gale was ever-present in the league, while his defensive partner Martin missed just two games and netted a memorable hat-trick against Newcastle in an 8-1 mauling of the Magpies in April 1986.

Martin ended his West Ham career with a total of 596 appearances. That achievement sees him sit proudly in fifth place in the club's list of all-time appearance makers. He also chipped in with 34 goals. Gale totalled 366 career appearances for the Hammers and scored seven goals.

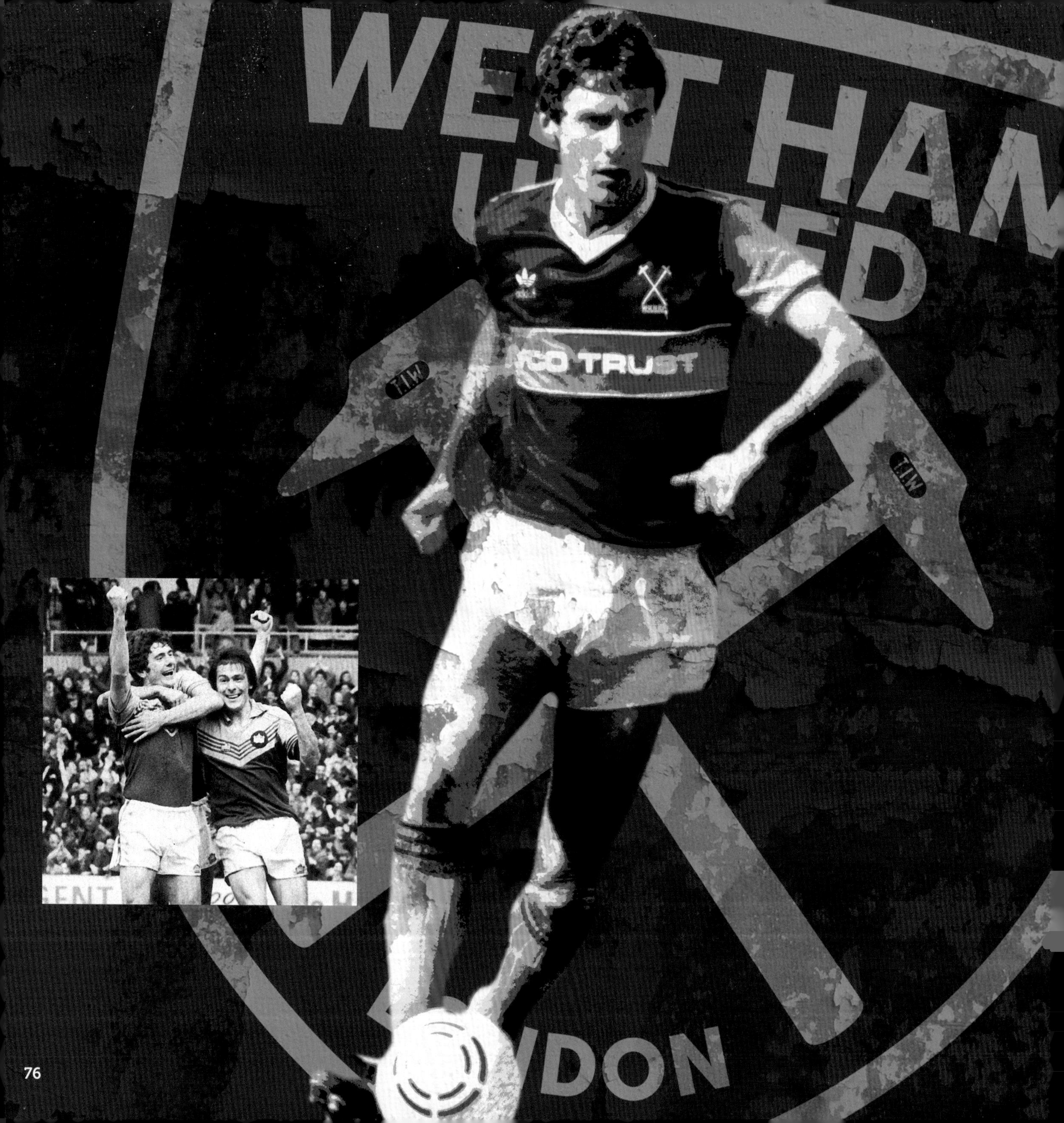
CO TRUST

CULT *heroes*
RAY STEWART

Ace penalty taker and FA Cup winner, Ray Stewart played 432 times for the Hammers over a 12-year spell from 1979 to 1991.

Born on 7 September 1959 in Stanley, Perthshire, Stewart began his playing career with Dundee United, joining them in May 1973. A promising young schoolboy prospect, Stewart turned down several clubs, including Scottish giants Glasgow Rangers, to begin his career at Tannadice Park. He was rewarded with a first-team debut prior to his 17th birthday and was handed the unenviable task of marking Kenny Dalglish during his first outing for the club.

After three impressive seasons with Dundee United, he came to the attention of a host of clubs south of the border and the Hammers' initial bid of £175,000 was turned down, before a fee of £430,000 was agreed in 1979, making him the most expensive teenage footballer at the time.

The first of those 432 outings for the Hammers came in a League Cup tie away to Barnsley on 4 September 1979. Stewart scored an amazing 84 goals for West Ham despite playing a right-back - this was due to his incredibly successful record from the penalty spot. Of those 84 goals, 76 were successful spot-kicks and three of the other eight are believed to have come from rebounds, once the 'keeper has repelled his initial effort from 12 yards.

Hammers fans are sure to have their favourites, but two standout Stewart spot-kicks that always come to mind are, the FA Cup quarter-final against Aston Villa and the 1981 League Cup Final against Liverpool. Both were high pressure spot-kicks, but both were crashed them home Stewart-style, to the sheer delight of the West Ham faithful .

Stewart's name is understandably referred to whenever the subject of great penalty-takers is mentioned, but regardless of his fantastic ability from the spot, he was also an outstanding right-back and a fully-committed defender who always timed his tackles to perfection. He was an integral part of many successful West Ham sides throughout the 1980s and his passion was rewarded with ten caps for Scotland.

A vital member of the club's 1980 FA Cup winning team, Stewart is notable for being the only non-English player to appear for the Hammers in any of their three FA Cup final successes. After injury called time on his Hammers career, he returned to Scotland playing briefly for St Johnstone and Stirling Albion. He later managed at Livingston, Stirling Albion and Forfar.

LADIES SQUAD 16/17

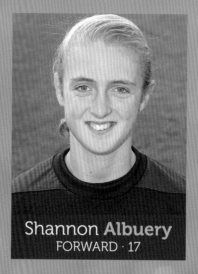

Shannon Albuery
FORWARD · 17

Stephanie Bent
MIDFIELD · 20

The **Management** Team
GREG DE CARNYS, KAREN RAY AND JOSH EWENS

The past twelve months have proved to be a hugely significant year for the Ladies. First, the Hammers enjoyed a historic 1-0 victory over arch-rivals Tottenham Hotspur at the Boleyn Ground, followed by the further good news that the Ladies' were being bought back into the West Ham family.

The undisputed highlight on the pitch was most-certainly the Ladies' triumph over rivals Spurs - a fitting farewell to the Boleyn Ground.

In front of a bumper crowd, the Hammers more than rose to the occasion as they earned a hard-fought battle thanks to Katie Bottom's powerful penalty.

Following a difficult start to the new season, the West Ham United Ladies have been brought back into the Club, following a period of time run by a third party.

Celebrating their 25th anniversary, the Ladies have been working closely with the Club and the teams will now work in unison to ensure the delivery of these and help maintain their continued progression.

As part of the move, Academy Head of Performance Greg De Carnys took over as manager, assisted by Josh Ewens and Karen Ray, and the new management team made an instant impact securing a vital 2-1 away win over Cheltenham Town.

The move will also see the West Ham Ladies Academy set-up, which includes Under-10, 12, 14 and 16 age groups, fully operated by West Ham United.

West Ham United Ladies will also benefit from direct association with the West Ham badge further cementing their association with the Irons, as well as the expertise and knowledge of the Club's administrative and football staff.

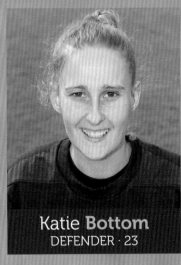

Katie Bottom
DEFENDER · 23

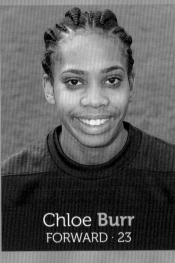

Chloe Burr
FORWARD · 23

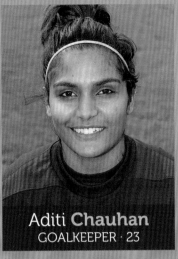

Aditi Chauhan
GOALKEEPER · 23

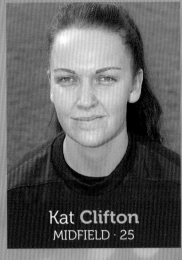

Kat Clifton
MIDFIELD · 25

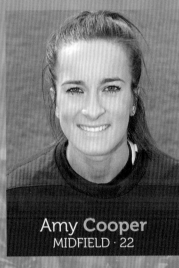

Amy Cooper
MIDFIELD · 22

Sasha Kelly
FORWARD · 25

Whitney Locke
FORWARD · 24

Chantelle Mackie
DEFENDER · 21

Jasmin Auguste
DEFENDER · 23

Dayna Chong
MIDFIELD · 20

Beth Griffiths
GOALKEEPER · 23

Olivia Sammons
DEFENDER · 20

Hannah Wheeler
DEFENDER · 18

Sarah Wilson
FORWARD · 17

This was Alan Pardew's second full season in charge at the Boleyn Ground

Given the clues, can you...

SPOT THE SEASON

WEST HAM UNITED LONDON

Striker Dean Ashton was signed from Norwich City

ANSWER ON PAGE 82

Also in this season, two clubs opened new stadiums - Coventry City (Ricoh Arena) and Swansea City (Liberty Stadium), Wigan Athletic won promotion to the top-flight for the first time in their history, England legend Paul Gascoigne took charge of Conference North club Kettering Town,

...and newly-promoted West Ham finished ninth and qualified for Europe.

The club bowed out of the Carling Cup away to Bolton Wanderers

Danny Gabbidon became the first Welshman to be voted Hammer of the Year

Teddy Sheringham scored the club's first goal of the season

81

ANSWERS

PAGE 56 · 2015/16 QUIZ OF THE YEAR

1. Juventus
2. Leicester City
3. Norwich City
4. Eight
5. Leicester City
6. Darren Randolph
7. Victor Moses
8. Wolves
9. Andy Carroll for WHU v Arsenal and Callum Wilson for Bournemouth v WHU
10. Mark Noble,
11. Liverpool
12. Michail Antonio
13. Leeds United,
14. Dimitri Payet - three
15. Eight
16. Nine,
17. Less than 66 - it was 65
18. Michail Antonio,
19. False
20. Winston Reid v Manchester United.

PAGE 68 · FAN'TASTIC

Bob Bradley
Slaven Bilic
David Moyes,
Aitor Karanka
Claudio Ranieri
Eddie Howe,
Jose Mourinho
Arsene Wenger.